Half Past Perfect

HALF PAST PERFECT

Writing Simple, Personal Stories to Re-Story Your Life

by
Barbara Allen Burke and Elizabeth Taylor

STORY PRESS

LAKE OSWEGO
OREGON

Half Past Perfect: Writing Simple, Personal Stories to "Restory" Your Life. ©2006 Past Perfect, LLC.

Printed and bound in the United States of America. All rights reserved. No part of this book may be reproduced or transmitted in any form or by any means, electronic or mechanical, including photocopying, recording, or by an information storage and retrieval system–except by a reviewer who may quote brief passages in a review to be printed in a magazine, newpaper, or on the Web–without permission in writing from the publisher. For information, please contact Z-Story Press, P. O. Box 284, Lake Oswego, OR 97034, or visit www.z-storypress.com.

Although the authors and the publisher have made every effort to ensure the accuracy and completeness of the information in this book, we assume no responsibility for errors, inaccuracies, omissions, or any inconsistency herein. Any slights of people, places or organizations are unintentional. Readers should use their own judgment or consult a professional for the specific applications of the information in this book to their individual situations. We assume no responsibility for how readers choose to use this information.

First printing 2006.

Visit our Web site at www.pastperfectstories.com for information on more resources for life story writers.

ISBN-13: 978-0-0779195-0-5
ISBN-10: 0-9779195-0-1

LCCN 2006902628

Attention corporations, universities, colleges, and professional organizations: Quantity discounts are available on bulk purchases of this book. Special books or book excerpts can also be created to fit specific needs. For information, please contact **Z-Story Press**, P. O. Box 284, Lake Oswego, OR 97034.

Dedication

To Granny, Hilda Taylor (1893-1972), who provided a simple world for me to connect to my heritage.

To Michael, for respecting my journey.

To my partner, Barbara–the perfect fit with me as a writer, a friend, and someone who will do the banking and the taxes.

To the souls who have traveled with me and whose stories are now woven through my own.

–Elizabeth Taylor

To my grandmother, Helen Farris, whose stories started me on this path.

To my partner, Elizabeth, for her generosity of spirit, her wisdom, and her unending pot of coffee.

To my children, Katherine, Sam, Kate and Sarah, who have listened to and believed in my stories from the start.

And, finally, to my husband, Doug, who understands why it matters, and for helping me check an item off my list.

–Barbara Allen Burke

TABLE OF CONTENTS

Introduction	13
Chapter One: Berry Juice and Blood	17
Waxed Paper	21
Chapter Two: Chalk Dust	23
My Young Heart	31
Chapter Three: Mythic Proportions	33
Camp Status	40
Chapter Four: Re-Story Your Past	43
Toys	52
Chapter Five: Throw Me A Lifeline	55
Beach Bags	62
Chapter Six: Kid in a Candy Store	63
The Rapture Comes on Sunday	75
Chapter Seven: The Paper Affair	79
The Last Gift	84
Chapter Eight: Play-Writing	87
Welcomed by Witches	99
Chapter Nine: Don't Duck Trouble	101
The Boy in the Mirror	105
Chapter Ten: Creating Heritage	107
The Phone Call	115
Chapter Eleven: Now What?	119
Moonshine	125
Chapter Twelve: The Last Word	129
A Daughter Walking Away	133
Bibliography	135
Recommended Reading List	139

From: Caroline Beckwith<carolbunnie2@internet.com>
To: Marsha Beckwith <mbmom@internet.com>
Date: Wed, 04 Jan 2006 22:09:25-0800
Subject: Your tuition dollars at work

Hey Mama,

Just got back from class. I swear my psych. professor is driving me INSANE (no pun intended). He asks us to read a chapter from the textbook, and then all he does is REPEAT TO US WHAT WE JUST READ! If class was just parroting back the reading, why do we need a teacher? It's so frustrating. I haven't needed anyone to read to me since I was little and you read me Good Night, Moon! Seriously!

On the plus side, I'm wearing cute shoes.

Love, the Bunwich

From the Desk Of Liz:

June 16, 2005

Dear Mom,
Thank you for the birthday gift. One can never have too many bars of soap—especially since I usually bathe with tiny cakes that Michael has liberated from hotels around the country.

Love your sweet and clean daughter,

Liz

To Do List - Tuesday

Call plumber
Make Sarah's lunch
Walk the dog
Coffee with Doug
Yoga class
Schedule pedicure
Clean litter box
Pick up dry cleaning
Arrange meeting with Liz
Edit Chapter Five
Buy split peas for soup
Drive Sarah to piano lesson

Peter--

Thanks for babysitting. Some more tips for watching the kids:
- Jason was up late last night and should be in bed by 8:00. That won't be pretty.
- Janie will beg you for ice cream, but she's already bouncing off the walls from too much sugar.
- Be careful not to let Tommy overfeed the dog. He's already thrown up twice today -- the dog, not Tommy.
- Pizza is in the oven. You'll have to pick the tomatoes off of Tommy's piece.

We should be back by 10:30. Call me on my cell if you need anything.

Grace

INTRODUCTION

You write about your life every day. No one expects perfection from emails, notes or quick lists, yet they accomplish their purpose.

An email conveys basic information in a concise and entertaining way in order to connect to the reader.

A thank you note pins a feeling to paper. (You decide if it is gratitude or sarcasm.)

A To Do list–although in outline form–gives a picture of the daily experience of the person who wrote it. You can tell from our example that the writer is a pet-owner, a parent, a writer, and someone with chipped nail polish on her toes.

And the note to the babysitter? What parents wouldn't be reminded of the glories and trials of their children's early lives if they found this note years later?

You document your life constantly through letters, emails, date books and notes. You might even keep a journal. These personal writings are the record of who you are.

Half Past Perfect

Writing stories from your past is another form of personal writing. It lets other people know what you've been up to. The only difference is that writing a story creates a meaningful pattern out of an array of details. You choose *which* details to share.

As storyteller Jimmy Neil Smith said, "[w]hatever their nature, stories begin and have always begun, quite simply; with a moment, an experience, a feeling."

Consider this moment captured by Elizabeth:

> *In 1959, Robin was a third grader. I, a year younger, had frizzy red hair and envied her long brown curls and tiny frame. At school, Robin was often first in line as a reward for being good. I used to look up from the main floor and see her pale white skin light up the dreary wood-paneled stairwell while she waited to be dismissed.*
>
> *One day our teacher told us that Robin had died. We were given no details, no grief counseling. The students were expected to carry on and not talk about it. But every day, I looked up at the landing, expecting to see her. Being dead was too scary to be true. How could someone so pretty and so good be gone forever? Where, my seven-year-old mind wanted to know, was Robin?*

Simple. Thirty seconds to read and not much longer to write; a small but significant recollection of Elizabeth's first brush with death.

All the impact of a moment can be captured in a few words. You have thousands of stories from your past, a lifetime of learning, poignant memories and

Introduction

milestones to revisit and record. Don't let that overwhelm you. You can take them one at a time.

The Power of Story is Our Story.

We came to personal writing from different directions. Barbara's grandparents worked in the gold mining towns of Colorado. After years of listening to her grandmother talk about mother lodes, cave-in's, high-grading and glory holes, she decided to record these stories. Using material gleaned through hours of interviews with her family, she recorded these events on paper. The finished book was both a Christmas present and a way to honor her grandmother's life.

Elizabeth began by writing one-paragraph vignettes for each year of her childhood. These quick stories recounted the most meaningful events she could remember. Annabelle, her 12-year-old daughter, read them and commented, "Mom, this is cool. Why haven't I ever heard any of this stuff before now?"

"Good point," Elizabeth replied. "You now know more about me than most people." After that, she realized how much of herself she had kept hidden. She was hooked on life writing.

We knew that we weren't the only ones interested in documenting personal stories. Lots of people want to honor their pasts. They want to be remembered, but often don't know how to begin.

Through our experiences mucking around in other

people's lives, we've come up with a little bit of "wisdom." This much we know is true:

- *Your stories are unique and worth telling.*
- *Everyone can write.*
- *Writing clarifies what you find meaningful.*
- *Life writing restores your past.*
- *Small stories are powerful.*
- *Anyone can publish.*

These are the ideas we will explore in this book. Notice we haven't said that stories have to be perfect to mean something. It's more fun to be half past perfect.

ONE

BERRY JUICE AND BLOOD

*I think we are made of stories.
When we die, that's what people
remember, the stories of our lives
and the stories that we told.*
RUTH STOTTER

Through writing about our lives, we assign significance to the past. "Story-ing" requires us to pay attention to our experiences. This is the unique authority of storytelling, which is embedded in every culture. Whether through pictures on a cave wall, Egyptian hieroglyphs, or the Dead Sea Scrolls, humans are drawn to share the events of their lives. Without stories, the links to our past would be broken.

Victor Frankl, a German psychologist, was imprisoned in a Nazi death camp during World War II. He lost everything, including his wife and most of his family.

As a result of his wartime experiences, Frankl developed *logotherapy*, a theory that a person's primary motivation is not the search for love or happiness. It is the search for meaning.

We are more than an accumulation of our days. Our activities, accomplishments, and even our suffering mean something. Writing clarifies what we are doing on this planet. It has the power to illuminate our purpose and communicate it to others.

Why then don't more people write their life stories?

Many of us will read the memoir of a film star or socialite but won't put our own experiences on paper. We often feel our lives are not important. Yet we acknowledge the value of a simple caveman's record left in berry juice and blood. The caveman obviously felt that his story about everyday life was worth telling, yet today's average citizen has lost sight of the value of recording personal history.

Even if you consider yourself an inexperienced writer, the power of story is available to you because you bring your emotions to the facts of an event. No one can write your life but you.

A life story is just an informal account of a subject about which you are already an expert. It is a relaxed form of memoir–a personal story *from* your life. Your tales can be one paragraph or one hundred pages; stand-alone stories or a series linked together to form a book.

Putting your memories on paper forces you to make

Berry Juice and Blood

decisions about how you view past events. *Choosing to tell an event one way and not another is the power you possess to create your personal history.* Storyteller Donald Davis wrote, "[t]he difference between telling what happened and telling a story about what happened is that instead of being a victim of our past, we become a master of it. We can't change our past, but we can change where we stand when we look at it."

You can choose to find different meaning in the same events. Marilyn Beyer, the author of "Waxed Paper," printed at the end of this chapter, chose a small moment from her childhood to write a powerful story. In doing so, she became the master of that event.

You have the opportunity to decide how to view your past. You can "re-story"–that is, restore your history. Naturalist Wendell Berry said that "[t]he past is our definition. We may strive, with good reason, to escape it, or to escape what is bad in it, but we will escape it only by adding something better to it."

Coming Full Circle

When you write a story, you assume that someone will read it. Your audience might be your family, a small circle of friends, or the public. Whether you print one copy from your computer or publish a book, it is up to you how you want to share yourself. The important thing is to begin, to gather your memories and wisdom and put them on paper.

Memoir is how we try to make sense of who we are, who we once were, and what values and heritage shaped us. If a writer seriously embarks on that quest, readers will be nourished by the journey.
WILLIAM ZINSSER

WAXED PAPER
By Marilyn Beyer

Like so many older people scarred by the Great Depression, Nanny, my grandmother, learned to make do with the little she had. She insisted we tear napkins in quarters. She taught us to pull Kleenexes apart to double their longevity. We were allowed only two squares of toilet paper. Nanny knew how to use sparingly, save and recycle.

This training came in handy in my large family. My father was a poor chicken farmer. There wasn't much money to waste on things like napkins, Kleenexes or toilet paper. Or waxed paper.

I don't know how old I was when I first noticed that most other children bought hot lunch at school. I found out much later that our family qualified for the free-lunch program, but my mother, chairman of the school board, was too proud to submit the paperwork. Instead, we brought lunches from home. Every day of my childhood, since I'd started school at age 6, I made my own sandwich before school. It was always peanut butter and jelly. I wrapped my sandwich in the leftover waxed liners of our cereal boxes.

I was in 5th grade when I realized that those who brought lunches from home had a new sack every day and sandwiches wrapped in real store-bought waxed paper.

It was a new school for me. I walked into the large, green cafeteria with rows of connected tables and benches and sat with new friends. Suddenly I felt embarrassed as I pulled out my peanut butter and jelly sandwich and carefully unwrapped the thick, pleated, seamed paper.

"What kind of paper is that?" asked my new friend, drawing attention to my poverty. From then on, I learned to open my sandwich inside the lunch sack, leaving the wrapping, and my fragile ego, carefully hidden inside.

I wonder how much money we saved using the waxed paper from cereal boxes for our sandwiches. I wonder how much it cost us in self-esteem.

The End

TWO

CHALK DUST

> *What we recall is not what we actually experienced, but rather a reconstruction of what we experienced that is consistent with our current goals and our knowledge of the world.*
> CHRIS WESTBURY AND DANIEL DENNETT

What makes some events memorable while others seem irretrievable? A number of significant events happened to Barbara when she was five years old: she started kindergarten, then moved from Colorado to Texas. Her youngest sister was born. Her father changed jobs twice. Her memories of these life events are vague. And yet, what stuck in her brain is the memory of hiding a pack of Dentyne gum, a treasure she'd hoped to horde, under the clunky radio that sat on her kitchen counter, only to have her mother discover it and share it with other children. How did that moment get hardwired into her brain while more significant events escaped her recollection?

For many years, experts believed that there was no brain structure directly associated with memory. Recent research, however, gives us clues about why and how memories are encoded, and what happens when we retrieve them. New technology allows researchers to look into a living, functioning brain. Neurologists and psychologists are now able to detect brain activity at the time memories are stored. What they've learned has applications for life writers.

Memories are not stored perfectly intact, just waiting for us to retrieve them. Given our computer age, we might think that our memories function like the biological equivalent of the CPU's of our computers. We assume that bits of information–say the scheduled time for your dentist appointment–are stored as files on a "brain" hard drive where they remain intact. When you need to retrieve that information, it's like pulling up a file: 10:30 on October 14th.

But computers, unlike our brains, don't relate facts to anything else. The human brain functions in a much richer, more complicated way. Human memories are not merely recorded, but *constructed* in response to an experience. Our memories are formed through the association of a number of facts. The time of your appointment is linked to the fact that your dentist's schedule usually runs a half-hour behind, and that the office always smells like Lysol, mint, and tooth polish. Different parts of the brain take note of the physical sensations and emotional impressions of the event, and establish a relationship between them to form a memory. Every time the relationship is recalled, it creates a "hard-wired" connection in the brain. The more often that memory is retrieved–such as the telephone number of the house you lived in growing up–the stronger that connection becomes and the more vivid and lasting that memory will be. As Ashish Ranpura explains in "How We Remember, and Why We Forget,"

> *When we experience an event, our brains tie the sights, smells, sounds and our own impressions together into a relationship. That relationship itself is the memory of the event.*

How does this affect life writers?

Facts are Filtered

Our brains select which facts are saved in order to be available for future recollection. For example, when you showed up for your first day of school, your senses took in thousands of pieces of information: the smell of chalk dust, the sounds of crayons waxed over pulpy paper, the teacher's voice and the tightness of your new shoes. Not all of the information made the cut. In order for that memory to be lasting, certain facts had to be selected and reinforced, while others were eliminated.

Although most people complain that they can't

remember everything, the function of selection is a good thing. It allows us to sort and categorize information. Being able to tune out non-relevant "stuff" enables us to focus on what we consider to be more valuable.

So what determines what gets saved and what gets pitched? Three factors:

1. ***Repetition.*** A piece of information – say the name of your kindergarten teacher – is repeated internally or externally enough times that the knowledge sticks.
2. ***Focus.*** Focusing your attention on something will increase its likelihood for recall. If you set out to remember your times tables or your best friend's birthday, chances are you will.
3. ***Emotional Arousal.*** Emotion focuses attention. To return to our first day of school example; whether you perceived it as scary or exciting will affect which aspects of the day you recall.

When you sit down to record an event as a story, the details that float to the surface are those that were reinforced in one or more of these ways.

These three factors are especially important for writers. What we feel about an event is associated in our memory with all the other factual data. The same facts with a different emotional overlay will elicit a very different recollection. If at five-years-old, we perceived the world to be a scary place, our memories of the first day of school will be different than if we were excited. Our stories will reflect our attitudes.

Sensory Memory

It is an obvious fact that the information we gather about an event comes primarily through our five senses: sight, sound, touch, taste and smell. It is less obvious how sensory detail is recorded and, later, recalled. Most people rely primarily on sight. When asked to describe someone, they will likely tell you what the person *looks* like.

However, when recalling a memory about an event or a person, all of our senses are clicking. Everyone has experienced the flood of memory that rushes in when we encounter a familiar smell. The smell of tuna or lilacs can evoke vivid, specific incidents or people, even decades after the fact. Furthermore, the sense of smell seems to be the most durable and powerful in provoking memory.

Once a memory is triggered by one sensory detail, the pathway is opened to invite memory from other senses. The more senses involved in the original event, the richer the recalled memory will be.

Sensory memory has a powerful impact on writing our personal histories. Recalling specific information from sight, sound, touch, taste and–especially–smell enables us to recapture the past. These very details used in your story--the taste of bitter coffee, the smell of pine trees, that song your uncle always played on the radio–will be the information that helps readers experience your past.

Memories Tell Us Who We Are

Our memories represent what we *believe* about our experiences. When we create memories, we include our emotional impressions as well as the *meaning* of each event. As neurologist Oliver Sacks wrote "[i]t may be said that each of us constructs and lives, a 'narrative,' and that this narrative is us, our identities." Our personalities, our sense of ourselves are bonded to our stories.

Elizabeth's story, "My Young Heart," printed in full at the end of this chapter, is about teen betrayal at a school dance. In it, Elizabeth describes a memory of her 13-year-old self:

> *I now stood alone, my baked-in-place grin getting older and faker by the minute. But girls didn't stomp off in those days. We pretended to have to go to the bathroom. We took refuge in makeup. Pink lipstick and black mascara kept the tears behind our eyes. We were all accomplished actresses.*

Elizabeth associated her memory of the dance with the potential for rejection. Although she eventually overcame the rejection, the feeling of it was forever linked with that night at the dance.

We are story-making creatures. Our ability to record, recall and relate events makes us human. Other animals –from fish to cats–make memories but no other animal converts them into stories.

Understood this way, our tales become more than just

lessons to be taught to children or entertaining anecdotes. *Our stories are the medium we use to tell ourselves and others who we are.*

Brain Stretch

Two final points of research are relevant for life writers. The first is a discovery regarding the brain's plasticity, which refers to its capacity for change. For years, researchers believed that brain development was most active through childhood and teenage years, but was essentially fixed by the time the individual reached young adulthood. Recently, scientists have learned that this assumption is wrong. Our brains continue to develop as long as we pursue intellectual challenges. Life writing is an activity that stretches and strengthens the brain.

Secondly, there is a bias toward remembering past events in a way that puts a positive spin on ourselves. This, too, is healthy. Explaining our history to ourselves in a positive light is associated with a number of health benefits, including improved immune function and quicker healing time, as well as reduced stress. Harvard psychologist Daniel Schacter quotes one researcher as follows:

> [O]ptimistic views of the self appear to promote mental health rather than undermine it. Far from functioning in an impaired . . . manner, people who are most susceptible to positive illusions generally do well in many aspects of their lives . . . Remembering the past in an overly positive manner may encourage us to

meet new challenges by promoting an overly optimistic view of the future, whereas remembering the past more accurately or negatively can leave us discouraged.

For centuries, people have been remembering their lives and recording them—on cave walls, parchment scrolls, and yellow legal pads. The process is not new. What is new for life writers is the understanding that our brains develop in ways that support storytelling. Reviewing our memories, re-visioning our pasts in a more productive and positive light, enables us to reclaim those events. The activity itself is healing, empowering us to seek a brighter future.

MY YOUNG HEART
By Elizabeth Taylor

It was 1966, the eighth-grade school dance. In the middle of January, Siberia-like weather blew across the Canadian prairies and Winnipeg was crisp at thirty below zero. When I entered the gym, I felt my frozen cheeks and nyloned legs begin to tingle with the abrupt change in temperature.

My red curls hung on the sleeveless shoulders of my safe, black velvet dress. Best friend, Pam, stood beside me. Her dark hair moved across the front of a green A-line dress as she executed the necessary survey for friends with whom we could hook up. Dances were scary without a gaggle of girls to share whispers while we all pretended not to be watching the boys.

Eric had zit-free Mediterranean skin and was a star hockey player. He was also my neighbor. Although we were friends outside of school, he rarely spoke to me during class. With this cool veneer, he was all the more attractive to me. I knew there was a sweet guy behind the aloof exterior. I prayed that he would ask me to slow dance and then walk me home. In my head, he'd already asked me to go steady.

"Pam," I said out of the corner of my mouth. "Eric's headed this way." I can still feel those sweet butterflies make mincemeat of my tummy. I had already noted his white shirt and beige khakis so I could pick him out of the crowd. I flicked a curl from my shoulder and looked the other way. The DJ was spinning "Unchained Melody." Perfect. Eric and I would sway in each other's arms to the Righteous Brothers' haunting tune.

Eric was three feet from my "yes" when he suddenly veered slightly to the right and asked Pam if she would like to dance. Pam, of course, had been well-versed in my crush. She was supposed to say "no." Instead, she glanced at me and shrugged before she took his hand. I watched this dual betrayal in slow motion while automatically replacing the shocked "O" my mouth had formed with a pasted smile.

I now stood alone, my baked-in-place grin getting older and faker by the minute. But girls didn't stomp off in those days. We pretended to have to go to the bathroom. Pink lipstick and black mascara kept the tears behind our eyes. We were all accomplished actresses.

Although I'd already run through several forms of torture that were too good for my ex-best friend, I knew in reality I'd just say, "no big deal" when we talked about it later.

When I returned to the gym, the final notes of the song were still in the air. I watched Eric hold Pam a little too close, a little too long. My stomach was now in the clutches of the demons that have haunted school dances since young women began to grace the doors of learning. I looked the other way. I pretended to wave to someone. I got over it.

Or did I?

A few years later, Eric became my boyfriend. "Unchained Melody" was certainly not our song–that was "Happy Together" by The Turtles. And although, like a sap, I had forgiven Pam, there was a corner of my heart that Eric could never own because of that dance.

The End

THREE

MYTHIC PROPORTIONS

There is nothing truer than myth.
EUGENE IONESCO

In 1200 B.C., many citizens of Greece and Asia Minor believed in a group of deities known as The Olympians. Through the rich stories of these immortals, Greek myth was born.

Beauty, poetry, and boundless creativity were bequeathed to us from the myth-makers. Perhaps the greatest gifts were the stories themselves–providing us a window to the origins of Western Civilization and brilliant examples of pure story. But myth abounds in all cultures.

We generally think of the word, "myth" as meaning, "false" or "untrue." Webster defines this word with far more scope:

Myth: a real or fictional story that appeals to the consciousness of a people by embodying its cultural ideas or by giving expressions to deep, commonly felt emotions.

The mythic story can be very real.

We are not writing about gods like Poseidon or Zeus. Nothing could be more real than our grounded, mortal lives. And yet, our stories will have a mythic quality. Myth enters into our view of ourselves and therefore our writing because it appeals to our need to express deep, commonly felt emotions.

Your Myth

Experience is connected to myth. Being immersed in self-experience is living one's own myth, one's own life story . . . We are our own mythmakers, knowingly or unknowingly.
STANLEY KELEMAN

Documenting stories from your life is fun and reflective as well as healing. Yet, it is not for the timid once you understand the cathartic nature of recalling, transcribing and reading your own stories.

When you put a story on paper, the experience you had actually changes. You define the experience to be something and not something else. You choose certain words and not others to describe your circumstances and emotions. You select a voice and an attitude. These choices place boundaries on your experience. These boundaries shape your understanding of what happened. Although they are props, they convert your tale to a form easily shared with others. We call this form "story."

Your story is now a selective, one-sided version of an experience. We all know that there is more than one side to most tales. This is *your* version. Your mythic life begins when a memory leaves your head and lives in print. It is first created because you have defined your story in your terms.

But the myth grows…

Reader's Myth

When someone reads your story, that person takes your selected words, voice and attitude, and through his imagination, forms his version of your story. He brings to it his experiences and "filtering system," so now your story has morphed into *his* version of your story. Two versions now exist. This effect is multiplied with each new reader.

Take, for example, Shakespeare's drama of *Julius Caesar*. Shakespeare took an historical figure and defined Caeser by choosing the story elements that he believed best described this character. If my friend and I read this play, we might form two different views of Caeser. Anyone who has attended a high school literature class knows this to be true. I might think Caeser is a tyrant, yet my friend sees him as a hero. We both read the same words but our brains compute the information differently. In one classroom there might be as many as twenty-five versions of Caeser's character.

Between the cracks of words, voice and action, myth creeps into stories and takes on a life of its own, separate from actual facts or original intentions.

A more contemporary example is the myth of Jacqueline Kennedy Onassis.

For the last thirty years of her life, Jackie O. did not grant interviews. Nevertheless, people wrote about her. Whether she participated in unusual or mundane activities, her life in print took on mythic proportions. It became more, rather than less, fascinating to us when she was, in fact, living the life of a private senior citizen. Why? Because she became a myth. We are far more interested in the mythical Jackie than the actual person. People took the basic, public facts of her life and layered them with their own emotional reactions to her. She became the person who spoke to our communal needs; the woman who personified our hopes and dreams for America; the woman who filtered through our collective and singular versions of (mythical) Camelot. That was the Jackie we knew. After all, Jackie made sure we never knew the real person.

You will find as you allow others to read about your loves, adventures, careers and regrets that people are drawn to the commonality of the human condition. Your story connects to the stories of other people. Curiosity compels us to know how another person has dealt with a situation we have had or might yet encounter. Stories put the human condition on the table. But they change the actual event. The more your life is written about, the more mythical it becomes. This is not a bad thing. On the contrary, myth shares elements that allow people to better understand themselves and others, which is, after all, the point of life stories.

There are two specific elements that transport a story into the mythic realm: imagination and exaggeration.

Imagination

> *The moment there is imagination, there is myth.*
> CAMILLE PAGLIA

Imagination is part of the magic of story. In imagining, we visualize events, conjure colorful pictures no other person can see. Our imaginations supply the details that make stories come alive.

An honest account of your experiences is the essence of life writing. However, to bring the full color and texture to your prose, you will use your imagination in two ways. First, when writing about an event, you call forth the "images" you have connected to it: the colors, tastes, sounds, and smells.

For example, "Camp Status," printed at the end of

this chapter, is a story handed down to Elizabeth from her father-in-law, Simon Klachefsky. Through years of retelling, there are now mythic elements to it. Although Elizabeth wrote it, it is told from Simon's point of view. It portrays Simon's reaction to the introduction of Polish prisoners to the concentration camp where Simon was detained during World War II. The story includes firsthand details shared with her about the event, such as the black and white striped uniforms, and the Germans separating Jewish families as they stepped off airless cattle cars.

She also used her imagination to create the details, now lost to memory, that make the story more real. Elizabeth wasn't in the Camp. She had to take the basic structure of what happened and clothe it with images that allow the reader to visualize the event more clearly. These details, factual or not, help communicate the essential truth of the tale. For example, there was an actual German guard in Simon's experience. However, Simon never described him. In order to bring him to life, Elizabeth imagined his appearance, giving him shiny red hair. Including this detail enhances the truth without changing it. Using your imagination, while embellishing your work, serves to bridge the gaps from truth to truth.

The next level of imagination takes place when the reader absorbs your story, and imagines it anew. Another creamy rich layer of myth is created. As Robert Fulgham wrote, "I believe that imagination is stronger than knowledge. That myth is more potent than history. That dreams are more powerful than facts."

Exaggeration

Another key element of myth is exaggeration. Writers use this tool in order to communicate a theme, an action or a lesson to their readers.

What happens when something is exaggerated? It becomes larger than life, larger than the facts and therefore more easily seen by the reader. Exaggeration pares down the fine details in order to accentuate the main characteristics.

For example, in "Camp Status" there are only two characters – Simon and Fredrich, the guard. Zooming in on two people, out of thousands who inhabited the Camp, exaggerates their roles as a prisoner and guard. In this mythic environment it is easier to recognize the common attributes of joy, misery, love, regret, or, in this story, revenge.

When you write your stories, do not shy from using the elements of myth to communicate them. In myth your work becomes compelling to your audience. In myth you leave the mundane. In myth your story is shared. As Philippe Lejeune said, "[m]emory's myth-making is necessary to life."

In writing, your life will take on mythic proportions because in the writing, your myth will grow. Stories beget myths, which beget legends.

CAMP STATUS
By Elizabeth Taylor

When we were herded out of our neighborhoods, most Poles made no secret of the fact that they wanted us gone—a polite way of saying "dead." They stood by while doomed Jewish souls fought to the last man and woman in the Warsaw Ghetto Uprising.

We got the news of the massacre here at Auschwitz. The Germans couldn't keep their mouths shut, gloating about the Jewish death-tally.

Then the Polish Underground suffered an unsuccessful uprising. They waited until the Russians were perched at the gates of Warsaw, ready to invade Poland and fight the Germans, under the mistaken impression that the Russians would help their fascist cause. Ha! Instead, the Russians watched the Germans squelch the rebellion, glad they didn't have to mop up the mess themselves.

I'd already had three years in Hitler's Hotel. My family had been captured, stuffed at gunpoint into a cattle car and shipped here pretty much when the doors opened for business. As prisoners arrived, the Germans separated them into two lines—Life and Death. My mother, father and sister...well, they were in line for heaven—if it exists.

My one hundred pounds of bones and not much else know more than any Pole. I am a wise old man of twenty, for to survive I've had to do unspeakable things—tasks no German would stoop to do.

I collect clothes from new Jewish prisoners as they are stripped and handed the black and white striped uniforms. To finger the fabric of a man who will die of starvation if he doesn't take a one-way walk to the ovens; praying for rich lumps in the lining of his pants—the wedding band, the watch, the locket—fills me with self-loathing.

But it is better than death.

Or is it?

Mythic Proportions

I am a dog who only cares about the next meal, the next breath.

I trade the jewels I can steal for food, liquor, cigarettes—for my heart to beat one more day.

In 1944 Polish prisoners began to trickle into this hellhole. The Clothing Collection workers were told that these prisoners could keep their own clothes. They could strut around the Camp with each other looking...well, like they were going out for a cup of coffee with a friend. The Germans had bestowed status on these traitors to make sure we Jews knew we were the lowest of the low.

To say that this bothered me as much as watching the Germans starve or kill my fellow Jews is to speak a sickening truth.

But I know things.

I know the Germans are a clean race. They don't go near the garbage, the bugs, the germs—the belly side of camp life. Most of all, they don't come into the Jewish sleeping cabins because they are terrified of lice.

So, it was a simple matter for me to whisper in the ear of Fredrich, a German guard. I drop a tidbit of information his way now and then and he gives me a smoke. Yesterday, the August light was sharp, making his red hair shine like a new penny. He bragged that he'd just had sex with a Polish prisoner.

"Lucky man, my friend," I said, nodding. "I would be envious but..."

His sucked smoke into his lungs and eyed me, squinting in the sun. "But what? Ha! You don't have sex. You never will, Simon Jew." He clapped my back. "Of course you are envious of my good fortune."

"Fredrich. You've been good to me. We smoke, sometimes we share a sip of schnapps. I am aware of your...uh...generosity."

Fredrich blew smoke rings, nodding.

"So," I continued, "it is with respect that I tell you—"

"What? What is it?"

"The Pole you had sex with—"

"Not your business," he said, frowning. "Besides, you don't know

her."

"No, but she's not...they're not... clean," I said.

"You mean–she has the...what is the word? Clap? A disease? But how could you know this?"

I leaned in closer. "All the Poles have lice."

"No." He shook his head. "They have clean barracks. They are not with you dirty Jews. We let them bathe. Give them soap."

"Oh, I know you do your best. It isn't the fault of the...uh... hardworking Germans. It's..."

"What, man?" Fredrich hung on my words like a frightened child.

"Their clothes. They bring the lice in on their clothes. And because they are allowed to keep them–to wear them everyday in the camp– well, the infestation grows at an alarming rate. The Jews have clean new uniforms but the Poles..." I shrugged. "Just be careful."

I left Fredrich scratching his head, his chest, his private parts; picking at his skin like a monkey.

This morning, the guards made all the Poles strip naked. They were de-liced and handed the black and whites.

Now they look just like us.

But they still know nothing.

The End

Four

Re-Story Your Past

> *One of the things that draws
> writers to writing is that they
> can get things right that they
> got wrong in real life by writing
> about them.*
> Tobias Wolff

The past is over. What's the point in revisiting it? No doubt, there were circumstances that were hard to live through and distressing to think about.

Recording your personal history with the advantage of mature perspective can heal old wounds. You can't change the actual events, or make believe they didn't happen. You can't lie. However, through writing, you can reframe the events in a way that is more positive. As storyteller Deena Metzger says,

> *Stories heal because we become whole through them. In the process of…discovering our story, we restore those parts of ourselves that have been scattered, hidden, suppressed, denied, distorted, forbidden.*

Writing our stories can literally change our memories and so gives us the power to change the emotions to which they were linked.

Subjective Truth

Life writing relies on memory, which is subjective and selective. We have all experienced times when our recollection of an event differs from another's. You swear your first date with your husband was at an Italian restaurant. He insists it was Chinese. What is the truth? Your memory of an event is colored by the way you process and store feelings and information about it.

That is not to say that your memories are not true. They are true for you. As storyteller Daniel Taylor says, "[t]rue does not mean factual (although it may be). True means accurately reflecting human experience." That doesn't mean you should deliberately mislead. Memoir writers must, in the words of Judith Barrington, "mine their experience, not their fantasies . . . to reveal the deeper truths of our lives and the human condition." Factual or not, your stories, honestly told, will have an emotional truth to them which is reflected on the pages of any memoir.

In addition, many writers have noted that once they

Re-Story Your Past

have written about their lives, their memories are forever replaced by the version told in their stories. They no longer can distinguish between their recollections and the stories based on those recollections. Through selecting which details to include in the story and which to discard, the writer frames the emotional meaning he or she attaches to that experience. Now a new imprint of the event is established in the writer's mind.

Mature Perspective

The current "you" affects your story. If you revisit the events of your past and examine them with the advantage of an older, more mature perspective, you can retell the stories with this new viewpoint that was missing when they actually took place. In doing so, you can restory your past, discovering fresh and previously hidden meanings.

This is not lying; not fabricating something that didn't happen. The divorce, the death, the lost job, still took place. But your understanding of that event has changed. You can see that rather than being a victim of your circumstances, you survived and learned and moved on. Your interpretation of the event is updated. When you write a story, the memory will be restored (and re-storied) to a form that is more emotionally true for the current "you."

Does this mean that all your stories will now seem happy, tied up with a pretty bow? Not at all! However, your memories may be transformed, imbued with new significance. The event hasn't changed. You just see it differently.

In the story "Toys" at the end of this chapter, Barbara wrote about childhood yearnings. The facts, as she lived them, were that there was little money, certainly not enough to buy toys. She remembered this fact as a loss.

> *I coveted the pretty babies of my friends—dolls who drank from bottles, wet their diapers, and closed their eyes when you laid them down.*

But in writing the story as an adult, her perspective shifts. She sees the events not only through her own eyes, but also through the eyes of her parents. That change is documented within the story.

Remain true to your "then" memories but know that time has played its part. Re-visiting our stories and spending time with our memories through writing leads us to an amazing aspect of life story writing.

Our stories give us choices. As storyteller Jack Maguire says, "[o]ur story constantly reminds us that we can and do make creative choices, not only in how we conduct our lives, but also in how we regard them and talk about them."

We have the choice about how we want to view our experiences. Our lives may be full of joy and sorrow, but the import of those emotions and the events linked to them are determined by what we tell ourselves about them. We have the opportunity to re-story our past in order to restore ourselves. That might take the form in writing of having a different attitude, reaching a forgiving state, being honest about a past abuse, or uncovering a secret that has affected your happiness. Re-storying has numerous faces. Restoration can take place in as many facets of your life as you wish to re-visit.

Can I Change My Past?

> *If the past has been an obstacle and a burden, knowledge of the past is the safest and surest emancipation.*
> LORD JOHN ACTON

Memories can be updated and re-created. I'll bet you're saying, "Yeah, right. If I play around with my memories, I'm lying to myself about what happened."

Not at all! Your memories are not necessarily "truthful," as in a faithful recording of events. When constructing a memory, you recall the gist of the situation, and how you felt about it at the time. It's a representation of your *belief* of what happened and therefore an honest recollection.

There are, of course, incontrovertible facts, both personal and on the world stage: the date your first child was born, or the morning of September 11, 2001. When writing your stories, you have an obligation to remain true to established, verifiable facts and details. For example, you wouldn't, in a story, relocate the World Trade Center Towers to Detroit.

Memoir writers have long dealt with this issue. In order to capture the meaning and power of a story, it's sometimes necessary to compress the timeline, to rearrange the chronology, or to limit the number of characters. And yet, writers have an unspoken agreement with their readers not to lie; to tweak the truth, not to fabricate it. Readers understand that some details are embellished, exaggerated or omitted. But they don't want to feel tricked. *The criterion is that you cannot change the events to the point that it is no longer your story.* For example, it is one thing to say you took courses at a college. It is another thing to say that you earned a degree if you did not. To do so would cross the line because it would not longer be a story from *your* life.

You can't lie. However, as we've discussed, there is room to move within the truth. How you remember your story is colored by what you believe about the event and the language you use to describe it. This shapes memory. If you want to reshape that memory, you must change your belief or use different words. Writing provides an avenue to examine your beliefs and language.

When you talk about your past, you recall the images from that time. When you share that recollection, you represent, or re-present, what happened, selecting words, tone and attitude. This is where you can make changes while retaining the integrity of the original facts. Here you have a chance to restore your memories by re-visioning–literally, re-seeing–what happened.

This is a tremendous opportunity. You can re-tell

Re-Story Your Past

the event in a way that provides the most meaning. New neural pathways are formed that, when recalled, become stronger. The re-creation becomes your new belief about what happened, which is no more or less "true" that any prior belief.

Life story writing is the mechanism by which you can review your past and rewire your brain in positive ways. As Jill Ker Conway writes,

> [I]t's important to scrutinize the plot you've internalized and find out whether it accurately represents what you want to be, because we tend to act out those life plots unless we think about them . . . We are time bound creatures. We experience life along a time-continuum; things happen sequentially in our lives, and we need to understand the causation. But we never really do understand it until we sit down and try to tell the story.

The opportunity to forge a new vision of yourself and others through writing, using the advantage of time and perspective, can lead to stronger relationships and a deeper understanding of all that has occurred in your life. You become better acquainted with yourself. As Ghandhi said, "[o]ur greatness lies not so much in being able to remake the world . . . as in being able to remake ourselves." You begin to see what you've been up to and why.

You don't need to be an expert on your life *before* you write about it. Life writing is a process through which you learn about yourself. As is true in many areas of our lives, the journey is as critical as the destination. The important thing is to start. Judith Barrington, in her book, *Writing The Memoir: from Truth to Art,* writes:

> *The memoirist need not necessarily know what she thinks about her subject, but she must be trying to find out; she may never arrive at a definitive verdict, but she must be willing to share her intellectual and emotional quest for answers.*

In Barrington's own memoir, *Lifesaving,* most of the action of the book describes her life in Spain as a young woman. However, the theme of the book is how she dealt with the grief of her parents' tragic drowning. The process of writing about her travels allowed her to re-story her emotions regarding her loss.

Similarly, Elizabeth Fuller chronicled her upbringing in Africa in her memoir *Don't Let's Go to the Dogs Tonight.* The story, told with dry humor and unsentimental prose, paints pictures of the dusty farms, dangerous wars and colorful characters from her childhood. Underlying this, however, is the sense that she wrote the book to work through her fear that she was responsible for the death of her baby sister.

Not all of your stories will be tragic. People also learn through pleasure and accomplishment. Either way, we guarantee that you have a story you need to tell. Perhaps you haven't identified it. Perhaps you haven't admitted that it's there; that it's *your* story. It needs to have the older

Re-Story Your Past

"you" lend it voice and perspective to enrich the experience of the younger "you." Listen for the voice. It's time for it to speak.

TOYS
By Barbara Allen Burke

It is days before my 40th birthday. You would think I'd be old enough not to be caught off-guard.

I receive a large cardboard package in the mail from my parents in Colorado. This doesn't surprise me. My mother always sends presents early.

I carry the box into my kitchen and set it on the counter, using a knife to slit through the packaging tape. I open the card. It has flowers and a printed message, wishing me the best in the coming year. Inside, my mother has written a short note:

> Happy Birthday, Honey.
> It's never too late to make amends.
>   Love you always, Mom & Dad

"Never too late?" I wonder. I have no idea what she means.

I dig into the box, tossing out packing paper. Inside is a soft-bodied doll with a porcelain head, hands and feet. She has short, blonde hair and blue eyes. The pink mouth is hand-painted and delicate. She's beautiful. I assume my mother sent it for my 6-year-old daughter, whose birthday is in a few weeks.

I call my mother.

"About the doll . . .," I ask. "Is it your present for Sarah?"

"No, honey," she says. "It's for you."

Suddenly, it all comes together. Standing in my kitchen, cradling the baby doll, I am completely undone.

My parents were teenagers when they married. They were poor, inexperienced and—eleven months later—the parents of a newborn:

Re-Story Your Past

me. Within five years, I had two sisters.

My sisters and I had clothes from a generous grandmother, and hand-me-downs from the people at church. There was food to eat. A special treat was a trip down Main Street to A&W for root beer floats. There were parks to play in, and somehow a Stingray bike to ride—one my father put together himself. But there were never a lot of toys.

I coveted the pretty babies of my friends--dolls who drank from bottles, wet their diapers, and closed their eyes when you laid them down; plastic dolls you could take into the bathtub with you.

Once I visited a friend's house. The walls of her room were lined with shelves full of dolls. She had dolls from Ireland, Sweden and France. She had a Native American doll with beaded moccasins and a fringed-leather dress. She had dolls with hand-painted faces and real human hair. I couldn't stop staring. I wasn't jealous, exactly. It just never occurred to me that I was the kind of person who would have such things. I was the kind of person whose parents sang songs on car trips, took us sledding on snowy days, and raked leaves into piles and let us jump into them. We just weren't a family with toys.

In the fourth grade, I made a rag doll out of a cotton sheet to earn my Girl Scout sewing badge. I embroidered a face with long eyelashes and made hair out of brown yarn. I stuffed her with cotton and sewed a simple dress. I named her—I was so original—Dolly. I was nine, and most of my friends had moved on to jewelry and nail polish. But I secretly slept with Dolly every night through grade school. Through junior high. Through high school. When I left for college, I finally packed her threadbare body into a box and moved away.

I grew up, earned degrees, held jobs, and married. Later, I divorced, and remarried, and built a blended family with four children. I bought all of them dolls. Katherine, the oldest, played with hers for a few minutes, tossed it in the closet and turned to her Legos. Ever the equal-opportunity parent, I bought dolls for our son,

Sam, until he started making them bungee-jump from tall buildings. Kate by-passed dolls altogether and went straight to stuffed animals. But Sarah, our youngest, loved her dolls. I was comforted, watching her play with them. We'd bring them on trips, and buy tea sets and black patent leather shoes with frilly socks. I relished her joy, and let it count for my own.

What pains me most looking back is not my own lack but my parents' heartbreak, knowing that their daughter longed for something they couldn't provide. They gave me so many other things that caused them great sacrifice—they bartered for piano lessons and scrimped for braces. But still, they knew. They knew.

And so, a few days before my 40th birthday, I get my doll. I name her Suzy. Sometimes, I let Sarah play with her if she is very, very careful.

The End

FIVE

THROW ME A LIFELINE

*If we respect the people we've loved, the places
we've lived, the issues we've championed,
the lessons we've learned, the jobs we've
performed and the feats we've accomplished,
then it's up to us to preserve them in stories
and to share these stories with others who
might benefit from knowing them.*
JACK MAGUIRE

How can you mine the stories from the vast array of your experiences? After all, you fill so many roles; you connect to so many people. It's daunting to know where to start, which story to choose.

To keep from being overwhelmed, it helps to apply a framework to sort your experiences into categories. To simplify the process, we've developed Lifelines. Lifelines represent seven of the most significant areas of your life: The Spirit, The Body, The Space, The People, The Work, The Play, and The Not. Using these categories allows you to narrow your focus, making it easier to identify your stories and gather information. Lifelines are a simple way to begin writing.

• *The Spirit:* This represents the core of your belief system–your spirituality, faith or personal philosophy. It includes abstract themes: values, ethics, responsibility, love, and faith. In this Lifeline you may reflect upon why you're here. Your internal spiritual journey is replete with stories.

• *The Body:* How do you see your physical self? How do you interact with others on this level? Your health, body image, and your relationship to food, exercise and sex all hold stories. Your connection to your physical being resides in this Lifeline.

• *The Space:* This Lifeline reflects where you've been. It includes everything from the environments you've experienced–cities, rural areas, mountains, beaches–to the spaces you've called home. Have you moved from place to place or have you been planted like a tree and grown deep roots? How has your movement or lack of it affected who you are? This Lifeline also includes the physical possessions with which you've shared space. Reflect on where you've passed time.

• *The People:* Your relationships to other people are central to many stories. You've had connections to parents, children, family members, romantic partners, co-workers, teachers, authority figures and peers. What tales can you weave about love and romance, or a favorite friend? Was there someone with whom you couldn't get along? The relationships formed with pets or other animals also fall into this Lifeline.

- *The Work:* Work is applied effort across your lifespan, and includes school, jobs and volunteer activities. When were you most engaged or challenged in your work? How did you feel about your chosen career or retirement? What accomplishments or failures need to be explored?

- *The Play:* Play is activity undertaken just for the joy of it. For some people, this is a sport or game. Others are interested in hobbies like reading, music, crafts, chess, and computer games. How have you engaged your mind and body in order to restore yourself?

- *The Not:* Although most people describe their lives in terms of what they have done, it is also important to explore life's omissions. What have you not done that you regret? What areas of absence do you wish you had filled: a lost relationship, a phone call you missed, a trip not taken, an apology overlooked, or a challenge unexplored? Often, meaning can be located in the blank parts of our lives, the roads not taken.

You may spend time thinking about some Lifelines more than others. Your past may have been dominated by a job–The Work–or immersed in family–The People. In some areas you simply draw a blank. Over time, the proportions of activities in each area may have changed. For example, relationships to other people shift with family responsibilities; recreational opportunities change when you retire. These observations may provide meaning.

Some stories overlap several Lifelines. For example, "Beach Bags," our end-of-chapter story, is primarily about The Play in the author's life. However, it also addresses The Body, The People, and The Space. Overlapping is okay. Just pick one area to start. It will likely be the area that most stimulates your memories. Using Lifelines, your stories will bubble to the surface.

Pay special attention to the sensory images your memories evoke. What were the smells, tastes, sounds, textures and sights that you associate with each event? As we discussed in Chapter Two, your senses provide a rich link to your past.

Lifelines are not meant to confine your tales. They are designed simply to help you identify them.

Story Starters

The next step is to gather some notes on paper. For this purpose, we have designed Story Starters, a companion notebook to jot down memories and explore story ideas. Its pages are divided into the seven Lifeline sections.

Each Lifeline section begins with a few pages of suggested questions to kick-start your memories. Read them over and see if they help. Jotting down the flashes of memory they generate will help you uncover the kernels of past events that might hold a story.

Throw Me A Lifeline

Sample Lifeline Introduction Page

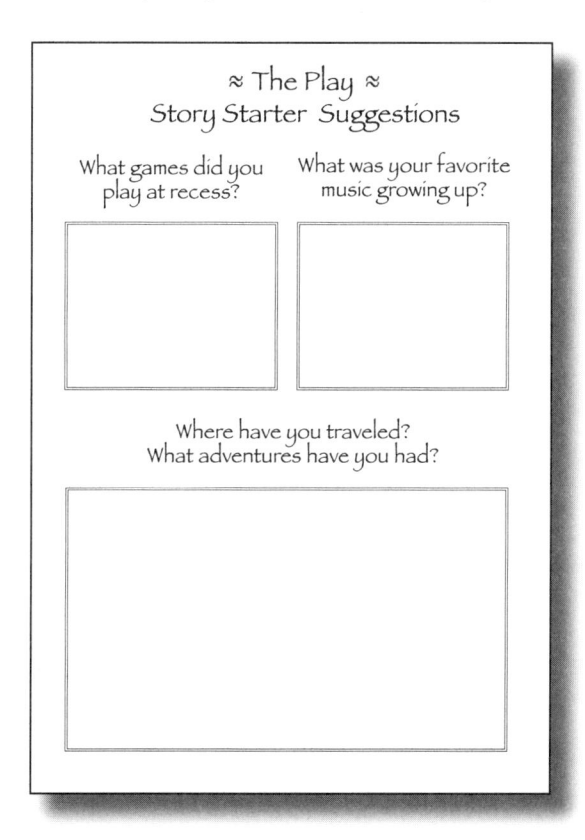

> ≈ The Play ≈
> Story Starter Suggestions
>
> What games did you play at recess?   What was your favorite music growing up?
>
> [   ]   [   ]
>
> Where have you traveled?
> What adventures have you had?
>
> [   ]

The rest of the pages of each Lifeline section are designed to help you flesh out the details of the events you'd like to deveop. The pages have boxes to identify specific information: when and where an event happened, and the people involved. For example, you'll want to locate the event in time. You can write your age, a general time period such as "high school," or "childhood."

Some people prefer to view their lives in terms of calendar years (the 1940's, the 1950's, the 1980's, etc.) or by more specific age breakdowns. Others might refer to an event (Prom Night or Retirement Party). It doesn't matter as long as it makes sense to you.

Fill out the boxes as indicated. The Notes section is used to record whatever other information comes to mind.

The author of "Beach Bags" used a similar brainstorming activity to write her story, as shown in this example:

Sample page from Story Starters

```
When?
Summer, 2000

Where?
Cannon Beach

Who?
Virginia, Patsy
Margaret, Flo

What?
--Went to the beach with V,
P, M & F
--Played Trivial Pursuit all
night
--Stay up all night talking
--Go back every year
```

THE PLAY

```
Notes--
   Beach Bags--
   no plans, no kids,
   just women
   easy meals, fires on the beach,
   taking care of each other, favors,
   Trivial Pursuit (Flo won)
   old lady jokes
   wearing sweats,
   pots and pots of coffee
   Patsy's casserole
```

Use the Story Starters notebook as a place to record

Throw Me A Lifeline

bits of memory. You might jot down a quote, or that flash of memory you had while walking the dog. For example, when thinking about the house where you once lived as a child, you could draw the floor plan. You might glue your 4th grade school picture to a page, or list your grade school teachers or friends. (Can you remember all of their names?) You'll be surprised by the oceans of memory these small streams open for you.

What you record on these pages are not fully formed stories; they are sketches, images, notes. Record those snippets: the smells, the tastes, the colors, the voices. This is pre-writing, which gives you the information you need to pen the story you wish to tell. Your notes don't have to be neat, well-written or even spelled correctly. This is a place to capture memories you do not want to lose.

You do not have to use the Story Starters notebook. You can develop your own system if you prefer: perhaps a box of 3x5 cards, or a notebook with dividers.

The more memories you uncover, the more you will find buried beneath them. Eventually, there will be one or two memories that will haunt you, demand that you think and write more. It's a fair bet that when this happens, you will have found the story you must write.

BEACH BAGS
by Carolee Carlson

The nickname evolved—a group of friends going to the coast for the weekend. Beach Bags.

No kids, no husbands, no menus. For a bunch of women with busy lives, it is heaven retreating into oblivion for a few days. Sleeping, guilt free, until noon. Meals are a conglomeration of whatever is on hand. Not planning is blissful.

The foundation of each weekend is generosity—chores accomplished magically, by someone else. Coffee brewed. Meals pulled together. Table set and cleared. Dishes washed. Trash taken out. Cocktails brought to you. Fire made. Music. Would you like a blanket? There is an inherent thoughtfulness among women. Heavenly.

Years ago, we stayed up all night playing Trivial Pursuit, drank beer, and laughed until we cried over nothing of consequence.

We've seen each other through a microcosm of life's events. Marriage, childbirth, divorce, careers made, stalled or abandoned, commiserating through our children's teen years. Today, many of us are grandmas. Our parents are aging; some have died. We've helped each other cope with cancer, arthritis, menopause, and hysterectomy.

Decades later, we maintain our annual getaway, a weekend of reminiscence and laughter. We can't stay up all night. Lacking enthusiasm for board games, we read or nap. Old stories, retold, are somehow still funny.

A disparate group, held together by bonds of sisterhood, we know each other's idiosyncrasies and love one another, regardless. It is Bagdom.

The End

Six

Kid in a Candy Store

What is past is prologue.
WILLIAM SHAKESPEARE

Within each Lifeline, thousands of stories teem, like minnows in a lake. Where to begin? You can evoke stories in many ways. What follows is a toolbox of techniques that can get you started. You may use one, two, or more. They all help you enter your story.

Perhaps you have tales to tell from The Space Lifeline. You identify different times by the homes you've had. Nancy Mairs, in *Remembering the Bone House*, chronicled all the places she lived and told what happened in those spaces. Did you have a tree house when you were a child or a place where you felt safe? Go to The Space Lifeline of your Story Starter and describe those memories. This activity may get you comfortable with putting story ideas on paper.

Here is a list of questions for each Lifeline that may inspire your writing. Consider them Story Starters for your memory.

The Spirit
- Do you have any stories involving religious institutions?
- Which books have influenced your spiritual life?
- What have been your experiences with prayer and meditation? What were the subjects of your prayers?
- What did you or your family do to help other people?
- What are your experiences with death–death of a pet, a loved one, an enemy?

The Body
- Your body has changed over the years through workout, puberty, childbirth, menopause, weight gain or loss, or illness. How did it affect you?
- What have been your experiences with food, sex, or drugs?
- What is the story of your hair?
- What were your favorite foods growing up?
- What outfit made you feel fabulous?
- How did you experience aging?
- Did you ever struggle with illness or disability?

- Do you have stories about body weight? Fat, dieting, eating disorders, or discrimination?
- What events contributed to your body image?

The Space
- What are the stories behind the homes in which you've lived? Can you list the addresses?
- How has your work space reflected your personality?
- What cars have you owned in different stages of your life? How have they or any other possession told a story about who you are?
- Are there parks, hotels, cottages or vacation homes that hold memories for you?
- What school classrooms spark fun or miserable memories?
- Has anything significant ever happened to you in a restaurant? A proposal or a break-up?
- Did you have a favorite toy growing up?

The People
- Which stories about your parents reflect how you feel about them and their influence on your life?
- What are your favorite memories about your children that you would like them to know?
- Did other relatives play a part in your growth? How?
- The people that you've called "friends" have influenced your life. What events or moments come to

mind?
- Co-workers have been jealous, helpful or encouraging in your work. Which ones taught you the most or had an impact on your career?
- How have strangers–people in passing–affected your life?
- Was there a relationship with a neighbor, minister, boss, employee, lover or teacher that turned your life around?
- Whom have you loved?

The Work
- How did you start working? Chores, a paper route, or babysitting?
- How did you decide upon your career?
- What jobs have you had as an adult?
- Which volunteer experiences meant something special? Work with children, animals, senior citizens, etc.?
- What part of parenting did you find gratifying? Frustrating? What would you want your children to know as they become parents?
- Do you have a stay-at-home mom or dad story?
- What are your gardening memories?
- College or school is work. What do you remember about it? A favorite class, life in a dorm, or student politics?

The Play
- What were your travel experiences? Ski trip, beach vacation, back-packing?
- What did you play at recess or after school? Dodge ball, four-square, jump rope, hopscotch, jacks? Make a list.
- What were your favorite games, hobbies and sports? How were they important to you at those stages of your life?
- What music transports you to earlier times? The Beatles? Frank Sinatra? Bon Jovi? Make a list of your favorite songs.
- Reading, antique shopping, walking or wine tasting are all examples of downtime activities. How do you choose to occupy your leisure time?
- How do you do nothing?

The Not
- You didn't marry Paul McCartney. You became a teacher instead of an astronaut. You had two kids, not the four you'd dreamed of having. You live in Florida when you yearn to be in Italy. What regrets do you carry through life? Should you have visited a dying friend? How did omissions and regrets shape you?
- Was there something you missed out on that was outside of your control? The toy you always wanted

but never owned, the job promotion given to someone else, the girl who never loved you back?
- Do your memories often involve what was missing from your life?

Using Story Starters may help you retrieve the more obvious memories. Some memories, however, are stubborn. To access these, you will need to be patient. The following tools will help you quiet the chatter in order to hear stories that speak in whispers.

Visualization

Visualization is a technique that allows you to create pictures in your mind. When you are relaxed and in a state of non-judgmental observation, you can capture elusive memories.

Sometimes these pictures relate to a story about which you are already thinking. Sometimes they will have nothing to do with any of your conscious thoughts. The point is to relax the mind and give it permission to create for no reason.

Select a time and place where you can be alone and in a quiet setting. You must be settled in order to hear your inner voice and to see clearly the pictures your mind creates.

Get comfortable.
Close your eyes.
Breathe deeply.

Visualize yourself in a desirable setting, such as lying on a warm beach or walking in a forest.

Allow yourself to "see" anything you imagine without criticism. Explore the pictures that float across your mind.

What do you see? Are images arranging themselves in front of you with details you'd forgotten? Let your mind wander. You will experience a feeling of detachment as if someone is simply showing you a series of slides.

Now, open your eyes...

Free Writing

Free writing is when you allow yourself to write whatever comes to mind in a stream-of-consciousness fashion. You may want to use one of your Freespace pages from your Story Starters notebook for this exercise. Write quickly, describing the pictures you've seen in your mind. Don't think about it. Don't edit or judge your work. Write for a few minutes, and then re-read your notes.

It doesn't matter what you wrote. You may use these notes for a story; you may not. You have sourced your subconscious treasure trove of thoughts, emotions and past experiences and your brain is in story mode–warmed-up to access your past. This is a quick way to kick-start your memories and, more importantly, to provide clues about which stories are trying to emerge.

The following is an example of a free writing exercise Barbara completed before writing "The Rapture Comes on Sunday," which is included at the end of this chapter.

Sample Freewriting Exercise

> Photos... Notes... Drawing... Freespace!
>
> That time I thought I was left behind the rest of my family. Racing through the house, starting to cry, feeling I was being punished for not obeying. Seeing things I thought were signs--dishwater still in the sink, Dad's magazine on the floor, things looking like they'd just been abandoned. My mind raced. How would I take care of myself? Get food? Medicine? Electricity and power and clothes. It was terrifying, even if only for about 15 minutes

Write to Photographs

How many of us have a trunk of photos filled with sepia strangers, begging us to tell their stories? They are destined to remain silent if no one takes action. Give your photos a voice. If you have pictures that need explanation or have interesting stories behind them, this is a great place to begin.

A manageable way to begin this process is to select the photos that are most important to you. Ask yourself:

- Who are the people in the photo?

- What's happening?
- What is the mood of the scene?
- What do you know about the setting?
- Is a "story behind the story" in this picture?

You can start by writing one paragraph snippets under a photo. This may evolve into longer stories. Either way, include what brought these people together–the place, the event, and the mood.

Find the Meaning

Martha Graham, a well-known dancer and choreographer, once said:

> *There is a vitality, a life-force, an energy, a quickening that is translated through you into action and because there is only one of you translated in all time, this expression is unique. And if you block it, it will never exist through any other medium and be lost.*

The uniqueness of your story makes it meaningful. Meaning makes your story worth writing. Without it, all you have is a blow-by-blow chronology of events.

E. M. Forster, in his book *Aspects of a Novel*, discusses the difference:

> *"The king died and then the queen died." This is a recitation of events. But, "the king died and then the queen died of grief." This is a story.*

The queen's grief is the *meaning* in the story.

You decide which stories are significant. They could be milestone events–the birth of a child, a marriage, the death of a parent. But small, poignant moments have as much impact–like the time the boy you had a crush on called your best friend.

The story you need to tell may be obvious. It may be buried deep within you. Listen closely until you find the one that resonates with you. The fact that it *matters to you* gives it emotional power to which other people will respond.

This process may seem straightforward until you begin to write. For example, there's an idea buzzing in your head. You ignore it and choose to write something else. It keeps buzzing, getting louder until the story you are writing seems trite and difficult. Why? *Because the other tale holds more meaning for you.*

We have a student who wanted to write about an interracial marriage in his family.

He began to write.

It was a good start.

But the buzzing in his head distracted him.

"Write about Dad," it said. "Write. About. Dad."

He finally listened and realized there was more meaning in writing about his relationship with his father.

Engage the Reader

Although the meaning provides the underlying structure of your tale, it's not obvious. Just as the foundation of a house is vital but unseen, the meaning is the silent guideline that steers your story lest you roam off topic.

But meaning alone is uninteresting. If you set about to tell your reader why an event is significant, you run the risk of being preachy or, worse, boring. *Messages become engaging when they're dressed in story.* As storyteller Robin Moore wrote, " [Y]ou must fashion [a story] and shape it, as you would a garment, to fit your frame."

One simple key makes your writing engaging: provide the detail that allows your reader to see or imagine the story along with you. Consider:

> *A chicken crossed the road*
> *or*
> *The brown chicken scratched its way across the gravel road.*

Which sentence is more interesting? A few well-placed details can conjure an image in a reader's mind. Keep in mind, we are not asking readers to see the chicken exactly as the writer sees it. We are asking readers to take these details and use their imaginations to recreate the chicken.

When most people set out to describe someone, it can sound like something you'd find in a police report. For example, John is a white man with brown hair, blue eyes and is about 5' 10. This description helps narrow down a field of suspects, but it does little to help us see the person as a unique individual who holds a toothpick in his teeth and stares at you from under the brim of a tattered Yankees ball cap. Or maybe John wears a Versace suit, slicks his hair back with pomade and fiddles with his Rolex watch when he's nervous. Depending on the details you choose, John can be a very different person.

Engaging tidbits will enrich your story.

In the end, choosing a story is about listening to your heart. If you're a kid in a candy story, how do you decide which treat to buy? Peanut M&M's or jellybeans? In the end, you pick the one you can't walk away from. Story starters, visualization, free-writing and photographs are all methods to connect to that unique energy that sparks the story you can't walk away from. Once you have found this story you will be able to find its meaning and share it. If *you* don't write your story, no one else will.

THE RAPTURE COMES ON SUNDAY
by Barbara Allen Burke

"Hey, Barbie!"

I heard my mother's stern Sunday voice calling. I ignored it and continued to rummage through the refrigerator.

"Barbara JoAnna Allen!"

Ooh. Now I was in trouble. I looked over the refrigerator door. My mother glared at me from the kitchen sink. I watched soap suds slide off her fingers into murky dishwater. "You get out of that refrigerator and get your chores done. Now move." *She started scrubbing a pan.* "I don't want to be late for the service."

My sister Karla stood beside her on a stool next to the drain board. She was still wearing her church clothes from the morning service and had a dishtowel wrapped around her waist. She looked over her shoulder and made a face at me.

I walked behind them on my way out of the kitchen and yanked the towel to the ground as I left.

I hung over the top of the corral fence, chin resting on crossed arms. Sunlight glinted off the horses' water trough. A breeze ruffled waist-high grass. It was one of the first really warm days of Spring. After four hours of choir practice, Sunday school, and the morning worship service, it felt good to be outside. Usually, the prospect of another two to three hours of church in the evening didn't bother me. I'd never known anything else.

Not today. Today the sunshine called. Today I was tempted to run barefoot through the field and tramp down a swath of grass to make a nest for myself. There I would lie on my back and watch clouds.

I climbed down from the fence and started back toward the house. Unaccustomed to my rebellious feelings, I slid deeper into them. *I deliberately scuffed my church shoes in the dirt. I stooped to gather a handful of stones from the gravel at my feet.*

"I hate church," I thought to myself. I threw a rock at the corral fence. It hit the wood railing with a thud. Anger had made me accurate.

I went in the back door, bracing for my parents to tell me to hurry. I was surprised by silence. I walked through the family room into the empty kitchen. Soap suds filled the sink. My sister's dishtowel lay on the stool by the drain board.

"Mom? Dad?" Where was everybody?

I hurried through the dining room—empty—and into the living room—also empty. My father's Car and Driver *magazine spilled onto the floor. My youngest sister's blocks sat in a messy pile in the corner.*

And then I knew with blinding clarity what had happened: The Rapture. The Lord had returned to call his faithful servants unto himself and I, Barbara JoAnna Allen, had been left behind. I could just picture it. While I was moping in the yard, my more righteous mother, father and sisters had been transformed into ghostly, light-filled figures and lifted straight to heaven.

I brushed away tears and trotted through the house, afraid to confirm what I already knew. The bedrooms were empty, the beds rumpled, closet doors open. I ran into my own bedroom and there, lying on the bed, were my Sunday clothes, set out by my mother. They accused me of my mean-mindedness and sloth. And now the Only Train Bound for Glory had come and I had missed it.

I walked more slowly, trying to remember all the sermons I had heard about the years of Tribulation that would follow the Rapture. I had to find a way to face it.

I headed toward the barn. Out of the corner of my eye, I saw something move. The family station wagon sat in its usual place. I stared. There in the car sat my parents in the front seat, facing each other, talking. My sister leaned out of the window.

"There she is," called Karla. "Are you coming or what? We're waiting, and the car's getting hot."

I didn't know what to do. I wanted to run and kiss my sisters' faces, curl up on my mother's lap and let her stroke my hair. I wanted to hug my dad and feel him hug me back. I wanted to laugh out loud. I wanted to apologize to God.

What I did was get in the car. It was time to go to church.

The End

Half Past Perfect

The destruction of the past is
perhaps the greatest of all crimes.
　　　　Simone Weil

Seven

The Paper Affair

*Getting involved in developing
and telling personal stories keeps
us from unfairly dismissing large
portions of our lives as boring,
routine or unremarkable.*
Jack Maguire

Now, it's time to write. For many people, facing the blank page is overwhelming.

Relax. We've made it simple.

The greatest thing about your life stories is that you were an eye witness to the events that you wish to transcribe. Get back "there" and remember how you felt when your best friend beat you out for cheerleader. What did the gym smell like? What was your friend's attitude? Did you want to rip her face off or just run from the school?

Worried about *how* to tell the story? The first step is to write it the way you remember it. If you've told the story out loud, write as if you were taking dictation. Get it on paper. If possible, do it in one sitting. Don't pause to fuss with word choice or spelling.

Allow your inner passion to get your point across. You don't have to force the process. You just have to get out of the way so the writing can happen. Remember, *passion is important because in our passions reside that which is meaningful to us.*

Secondly, think small. You don't have to write a book. Every story has its own length. Some can be told in one paragraph. Others require a few pages. There is significant power and substance in a short story.

Eventually, a number of short stories could be collected to form a book. The essence of a person's life can be represented in a series of vignettes.

"The Last Gift," a story printed at the end of this chapter, is Elizabeth's recollection of one of her father's last days. It is a two-page story describing a single powerful moment. She wrote the initial draft in one sitting. Although the story went through several revisions, the basic elements never changed.

Your first draft does not have to be perfect–just readable. In our workshops, many students read their work aloud and were encouraged that, although their grammar wasn't right out of *The Elements of Style*, their stories were powerful. Your true feelings will show up on the page through the words and pictures you create. Revision can be done later.

Remember, it is not the recounting of events that the reader is looking for, but a darn good story.

Voice Lessons

> [E]volving into better storytellers proceeds from listening and relistening . . . to ourselves, to what our deep memories and creative voices have to say to us once we've silenced our mind's surface chatter.
> JACK MAGUIRE

Your voice is your medium. It's what you hear in your head when you read–the author's fingerprint. Honestly recounting your stories, with feeling and emotion, will allow a clear path for your authentic voice. It may be edgy, sarcastic, funny or mysterious. Most of all, it must be true to who you are. Choose the voice that best communicates your story. It will be heard through your work, for you are the one who has something to say.

Dave Barry communicates through humor. Ivan Doig, who wrote *This House of Sky*, uses a poetic voice. Tobias Wolfe, in *A Boy's Life*, relies on a serious, straightforward tone.

The point is your writing should sound like you.

There is only one voice you must avoid: whining. It's boring. For instance, if you write a piece complaining that your friend hurt your feelings, the reader might wonder what your friend's side of the story would be instead of listening for your message. Use a different tone, such as humourous, and that story could work well.

Every life story you write will have a *then* and a *now* voice. The *then* voice has to be just that. If the story time is when you were ten years old, then the reader must hear the ten year-old.

Your *now* voice, when you choose to use it, provides wisdom and maturity. It lends perspective, which is an important aspect of life writing, because *your* voice, the author's, is allowed into the story.

When to use each voice? The story part of your writing will contain your *then* voice. When you want to jump out of the story and provide perspective, use the *now* voice. Perhaps the reader won't understand parts of the story without some clarification from you.

In "The Last Gift," Elizabeth returns to her experience as a 36-year-old woman. She chose to tell the entire story with her *then* voice, returning to how she felt when this event took place:

Too tired, too married, too pregnant.

Use strong words and communicate confidently. Even if, in your story, you were a vulnerable character, you are now a storyteller. A strong voice communicates the importance of your tale and the fact that it is a worthy

The Paper Affair

read.

One short story can capture a moment of life, a moment of the author's truth, on paper.

And that's all you are trying to do.

THE LAST GIFT
by Elizabeth Taylor

I sat on the edge of the bed threading my fingers through my father's pale hair. It used to be golden—the Taylor's crown.

"Remember when I was a child, Dad? I used to sit on the arm of your worn, brown chair, combing your hair while you watched baseball? You said it felt good, like a massage." A silly pastime, I thought now. But I'd have done anything for his attention. Little-girl longing flooded my throat and I could no longer speak.

Not that he'd notice.

Thank goodness. It made my task easier. I rummaged in my leather bag until I felt the small scissors. I stared at their gold edges, even as I shifted closer to Dad. His breathing was loud and labored, his head tilted to one side. It's no big deal, I thought, because he isn't really here. He's...in between addresses.

He'd never know...

I reached for a lock of his faded hair.

Please don't wake, I prayed. Please don't catch me. Doing what? Giving up on him, I supposed. I quickly snipped the parched strands. They fell into my hand like withered grass. Hairs that had been in place for so long now threatened to separate, like spaghetti freed from its box. My fingers pinched the dead wisps a little tighter.

It's done.

I returned the scissors to my bag and reached into the pocket of my raincoat. "April in Winnipeg. You're not missing a thing, Dad."

I extracted a piece of green ribbon and laid it across the bed, lining up the hair in an even little clump. With slow care, I tied a tight bow around my treasure. "Green is your best color. Remember that golf shirt with your name above the chest pocket? 'Gabe' in bright yellow letters. You had a sweet swing."

The Paper Affair

The peaceful droop of Dad's jaw seemed to agree.

I placed his hair in a white business envelope. Why hadn't I bought something thick and ivory-elegant with fancy ribbon to match? Instead, I'd scrounged around in my junk drawer and grabbed Christmas ribbon.

Right on cue, excuses echoed in my head, like a comforting cup of cocoa.

Too tired, too married, too pregnant.

I licked the sticky tip of the envelope, sealed it and tucked my father's last gift into my purse. Then I leaned over and kissed his cheek.

At the hospital room door, I turned and tried to memorize that face I would miss so much.

The End

Half Past Perfect

*I like to write when I feel spiteful;
it's like having a good sneeze.*
D. H. LAWRENCE

Eight

Play-Writing

In the past Americans spent time writing letters, journals and diaries. Wouldn't it be wonderful if Americans would once again write about their lives?
Lois Daniel

You've written your story. If you're satisfied with it, that's great! If, however, you still feel a little lost, keep reading and we'll show you how to Play-Write.

We use the term Play-Writing in two ways. First, have fun with your story; play with your writing. You are at your most creative when you enjoy what you're doing. In addition, when you play-write your story, you become the director of the limited world in which your story lives. You call the shots, set the mood, build a new reality for your audience.

There are only five simple elements you need to know

to play-write a story.

1. Opening Lines
2. Setting the Scene
3. Casting Call
4. The Drama
5. The Wrap

Before we discuss these elements, please read "Welcomed by Witches," printed at the end of the chapter. Our examples will refer to this story.

1. *Opening Lines*

The purpose of the first sentence of any story is *to hook the readers and to make them want to read the second sentence and the third.* You don't have to be a Pulitzer Prize winner to write a good opening line. You just have to know how to dangle a line. The following samples give you an idea of some intriguing first sentences:

> *Soon before daybreak on my sixth birthday, my mother's breathing wheezed more raggedly than ever, then quieted. Then stopped.*
> IVAN DOIG, This House of Sky

> *On a glittering August morning in 1979, at the edge of a salt marsh in Kennebunkport, Maine, I made a psychic sick.*
> NANCY MAIRS, Remembering the Bone House

Play-Writing

Summer, ninety-five degrees, the street in East Boston where the residence for chronic schizophrenics is sits dead and silent in the heat.
      Lauren Slater, Welcome To My Country

There are a few tricks to creating a good opening line. The first trick is to use sharp details (do we sound like we're nagging) so your readers can see your word-pictures. In the above examples, we are struck by the words *daybreak, wheezed, glittering, salt marsh, dead* and *silent.*

You also hook your reader by including something unexpected. In each example, the reader is enticed. There is a question left unanswered. Why did Ivan Doig's mother die? What did Nancy Mairs do to make a psychic sick? What was Lauren Slater doing with chronic schizophrenics?

A good first sentence might also hint at the subject of your story. This is nice but not necessary. The meaning doesn't have to be obvious. However, whatever you introduce in your opening lines should at least appear in your story. If, for example, you say something about your grandmother in your first sentence, she should show up in your tale.

Anyone can create opening lines. With practice you will be able to identify a good launch-phrase. If you've chosen a story you wish to write, jot down a few first sentences. Play with them, then re-read them. Is there one sentence that grabs your interest?

When writing "Welcomed by Witches," Elizabeth had many choices in creating an opening line. Consider these two options:

1. *I got ready to go to the play.*
2. *I dragged a brush through my robin-breast colored hair and zipped a pink lipstick across my lips to feign the energy that I definitely didn't feel.*

What makes the second sentence more interesting? It creates a word-picture for the reader. Details, such as the *robin-breast colored hair* and *pink lipstick*, make it easier to imagine the scene.

Also, the reader is left a bit off balance. Why is she getting ready to go somewhere when she feels so tired? To answer this, the reader must continue.

The simple way to know if you have a good opening line is to ask yourself if you would want to keep reading.

So, Opening Lines include:
- Details that paint pictures.
- Something which entices the reader.

2. Setting the Scene

Every story must set the reader in a time and place. This doesn't mean that you need to say, *"at 6:00 p.m. on May 16, 1982, I went to a play in Stratford-upon-Avon, England."* This information can be communicated indirectly by appealing to the senses.

Play-Writing

> *We pulled into Stratford-upon-Avon on a cool evening in May. Cruising down Main Street, it hadn't taken long to spy a quaint, Tudor-style hotel, the kind where you have to bend your head to walk through every doorway.*

In this example, the writer goes beyond basic facts to create the scene. You feel the "cool" air, you imagine the low doorways, you visualize the Tudor hotel.

In short, appeal to your reader's five senses:
- What did you smell?
- Hear?
- Taste?
- Touch?
- See?

3. Casting Call

We tell stories of people who weave through our lives and with whom we have shared experiences. For the purposes of a simple story, try to limit the actors to two or three. Doing so will help you focus on the stars of your story and avoid confusing your reader.

The actors may show up in different places. You might describe someone in your Opening Lines, when you Set the Scene, or in the main body of your story. Wherever they appear, it's helpful to know how to bring them to life.

The more you know about these people before you get started, the easier it will be to capture their images in words. It's handy to have a description of your actors nearby when you write. Refer to the notes you jotted in your Story Starters notebook. You don't have to use all the information, but it helps to "see" the person as you pen your story. Here is a list of triggers that might help you describe your characters:

> *Hair, eyes, smile, skin, blemishes, height, shape, quirks, bad habits, manners of speech, dress style, favorite possessions, activities, hobbies, grades, career, house, collections, type of car, attitudes towards others.*

Since you're writing about people you know (as opposed to imagined characters), it should be a simple matter to remember identifying details. For instance, you know that your best friend in high school hated Pepsi, your father wore golf shirts to work, and your sister stole your Beatles albums.

Don't forget that *you* are a part of the cast. You may be the star of your stories, so learn how to describe yourself. But how many selves have you had in your lifetime? The ten-year-old you is not the same as the fifty-year-old you. Describe the *you* about whom you are writing. Don't assume the reader knows the *you* to whom you refer.

For example, when Elizabeth wrote "Welcomed by Witches," she had the following list from her Story Starters notebook nearby:

Play-Writing

> Notes --
>
> Elizabeth
> - 29 years old
> - Robin-breast colored hair
> - Pink lipstick
> - Winks at cats
> - Blue jeans and white shirt/mustard stain
> - Sassy to brother
> - Likes English Lit.
> - Shakespeare groupie
> - Drinks English Breakfast tea with lemon
> - Adores Paul McCartney

Not only is the physical description noted, but Elizabeth's attitude is also emerging. She wears jeans and a mustard-stained t-shirt, so she probably doesn't mind what other people think (unless, of course, it's Paul McCartney). We know she has no problem speaking her mind because she sasses her brother. In addition, she likes cats but this detail didn't make the cut because it wasn't relevant. She chose the information most apt for her story.

To recap:
- Have description about each person handy as you write.
- Don't forget yourself. Use details from the period

of your life you are describing.
- Sprinkle these details throughout your story.

4. The Drama

This is the section where the writer tells what happens. It's the meat and potatoes of the tale. It is also where the reader learns why the writer feels the story is significant. Quite simply, The Drama is the action that happens between the beginning and the end of your story. What events made the story stand out in your mind?

You may find that you have much more action than you want to tackle. For example, the drama of "Welcomed by Witches" takes place over an entire evening, but not every moment was included. It didn't include the fact that Elizabeth was also traveling with her mother. Because her mother didn't attend the play, she wasn't included in the story. Also, there was more dialogue, much of which was omitted. The only conversations included were those that moved The Drama along.

How do you decide what to keep and what to leave out? It's your story. You decide which moments are most powerful. However, here are a few suggestions; clues to where meaning often resides.

You might make a quick outline in the "What" box of your Story Starter to identify the highlights. For example:

Play-Writing

> What?
>
> The Drama:
> 1. Found hotel
> 2. Raced to theatre
> 3. Bought tickets and found seats
> 4. Play brought back high school memories
> 5. Mesmerized by witches.

Forcing yourself to make an outline helps you identify the key action in your story.

Another way to isolate significant moments is to pay special attention to when the outcome of an event moves in an unexpected direction. It doesn't have to be a big shift. Small changes can be meaningful. For example, in "Witches," the shift is in Elizabeth's attitude over the course of the evening. She went from being harried and stressed to experiencing the "literary thrill" of seeing Shakespeare's Macbeth performed in the Bard's hometown. She is moved to another place. As she wrote, "the brilliance of the man . . . washed over me like a blessing."

Balance your writing between these three elements:

• *Narrative*–telling what happened. Try to stay away from general statements and stick with the specifics of your action.

• *Dialogue*–showing conversations. A little dialogue

goes a long way, but it's a powerful tool to bring your story to life. Dialogue should advance your story and tell something about the speaker. Don't worry if you can't remember conversations verbatim. Nobody can, and real-life conversations are tedious and repetitive. Hit the main points.

• *Reflection*–evaluating the meaning of what happened. Life writing allows you to include how you feel now about an event. Perspective is the part of a memoir where the storyteller can impose an older, wiser voice if he or she wishes.

In summary:
- Use an outline to identify The Drama.
- Pay attention to how the story or an actor changes from the beginning to the end.
- Balance narrative, dialogue and reflection.

5. *The Wrap*

A story must have an ending for the reader to feel satisfied. It doesn't have to end happily, nor does everything need to be resolved. It is acceptable to leave your readers wanting more. You do, however, need to bring the action to a close so that the reader can see the meaning of this specific event. When trying to wind up your tale, avoid general statements that can cheat the reader.

Here are several examples of endings for "Witches":

I sat in the balcony and watched the play.

Play-Writing

I sat in the balcony with Bruce and watched the play and thought about my high school English teacher.

The hair on my neck prickled as the hags bent over the boiling brew and chanted their immortal words.
  Double, double, toil and trouble.
  Fire burn and cauldron bubble.

The first example brings the action to a close, but gives the reader no idea what it meant to the writer.

The second ending brings the action to a close and gives some idea that the event was important, but the reader doesn't really know why.

The third example brings the action to a close in a specific moment, illustrating the significance of the event. The reader experiences the magic along with the writer.

To recap:
- Find a moment at which your story ends.
- Wrap up the action.
- Provide a glimpse at the meaning of your story.

"Welcomed by Witches," using under 500 words, and a little over one page of writing, illustrates a tiny slice of life. The author is not trying to tell you her whole life story, or even her entire day. She has captured one evening in England. *The story is in the detail.* All those scribbles and scratches that had been parked in the Story Starters notebook had done their job to bring to life that one evening. The five elements discussed in this chapter are covered in her story. Use these techniques to get your tales from memory to paper.

Play-Writing

WELCOMED BY WITCHES
by Elizabeth Taylor

I dragged a brush through my robin-breast colored hair and zipped a pink lipstick across my lips to feign the energy that I definitely didn't feel. We'd pulled into Stratford-upon-Avon on a cool evening in May. Cruising down the main street, it hadn't taken long to spy a quaint, Tudor-style hotel—the kind where you have to bend your head to walk through every doorway. The fact that people were much shorter five hundred years ago somehow translated into higher hotel tabs.

Before making our way up the tiny wooden staircase to our rooms, my brother, Bruce, and I learned from the concierge that the curtain was about to rise on a performance of Macbeth *at the Stratford-upon-Avon Theatre.*

"We gotta go now." Bruce opened the door to the narrow hallway. "We'll miss Act I. Come on." He frowned, his mouth tight with fatigue from a full day of trying not to kill us by driving on the left side of the road. He pulled his fingers through his blond hair.

"Do you know where to go?" I asked.

He rolled his eyes. "How hard can it be to find a theatre in Shakespeare's home town? My guess is Main Street."

"Or maybe," I said, walking past him, "you asked for directions."

We raced to the end of the street where the theatre stood beside the winding Avon River. A wide concrete staircase rippled out to the street in welcome.

I hoped our blue jeans would not offend the ancient spirits of the English stage or, more importantly, the ticket manager. But no dress code appeared to be in effect, as the ticket lady didn't glance twice at the mustard stain on my white T-shirt.

We found our seats in the left balcony. As the curtain rose, the witches cackled as horribly as the Bard must have imagined they would when he wrote them into existence. I silently thanked my eleventh grade teacher, Mr. Derraugh, for grilling us relentlessly on the multi-layered tragedy that is Macbeth. *The brilliance of the man who, hundreds of years ago, had lived and worked a mere few streets away from where I sat, washed over me like a blessing. I was as near to Shakespeare as I would ever be. If there ever was such a thing as a "literary thrill," this was it. The hair on my neck prickled as the Hags bent over their boiling brew and chanted their immortal words:*

> *"Double, double toil and trouble.*
> *Fire burn and cauldron bubble."*

The End

Nine

Don't Duck Trouble

*The real voyage of discovery is
not in seeking new lands but in
seeing with new eyes.*
Marcel Proust

Some people gain the most insight in difficult times. Conflict and hardship force us to struggle down unknown paths that we may prefer to avoid. But don't turn away from the tough memories too quickly. They provide drama and a wealth of wisdom that adds dimension to your stories.

Conflict can come from tragic issues, like death or divorce, or it can be small and very, very interesting. And yet, most people try to steer clear of difficult memories. They want others to feel good about a shared past or a family event. Stories seem so definite, so frighteningly "out there" when written on the page, especially if it's a story that another person may not want revealed.

Some people have disturbing tales to tell. "The Boy in the Mirror" by Steve Cobb, printed at the end of this chapter, is about a troubled teen Steve knew in his youth and the impact that person had on him. It wasn't a comfortable memory for Steve, but it held meaning.

Telling the truth about difficult times can illuminate issues that we want resolved or healed. The benefits to you and possibly to others could outweigh the drawbacks to keeping your story off the page. Bring it into the open air even if you are the only one who ever sees it. Addressing the conflict in story can be a positive step. As Isak Dineson wrote, "[a]ll sorrows can be borne if we put them into a story or tell a story about them."

How do you decide which conflict is appropriate to pursue on paper? Ask yourself two questions:

First, *is this my story to tell?* Most stories are shared and so can belong to more than one person. However, if telling your version helps you document or make sense of your experience, it is *your* story. If you were not an active participant in the event, or have not been invited to write about it, you might think about why you are telling it. Which leads us to the second question:

What are your motives in telling the story? Are they to extract the value and meaning from your experiences, or are you seeking to keep the conflict alive? Is it about healing or revenge? For example, your married neighbor flirted with you and you think that would be amusing to write. This is obviously your story since you are a participant. But think about why you want to tell it. Who would this story hurt? Certainly it would upset your neighbor's spouse. You may contribute to marital damage, nasty gossip and a certain breakdown in your relationship with this couple. And for what? So you can write what amounts to a gossip column? This helps no one.

Perhaps you have a difficult story. You believe it is yours to tell and your motive is to resolve a situation. However, you suspect that other people in the story may object to it being brought to light. You may have to grapple with your understanding of "loyalty" to family, to ideals, and to yourself. You need to be at peace with your conscience in your pursuit of the illumined truth.

There are alternatives. You can keep your writing private, or limit its circulation. You can give those about whom you write an opportunity to read and comment on your work. You can disguise the people in your story by changing names or identifying characteristics. If the issues are serious, you might want to discuss your choices with a professional.

Whatever you decide, honor the experiences you have lived. Difficult, sometimes tragic stories are a part of life, which are worthy of being documented with all their warts and beauty. Find a way to silence the voices of other people while you get your story down.

Judith Barrington says, "It is very difficult to be both candid and deceptive at the same time and a memoir needs to be candid. Tampering with the truth will lead you to writing a bit too carefully–which in turn will rob you of the ease that goes with honesty."

Your honesty illuminates the tough stories and imbues them with the power to push through the obstacles others might throw in your way.

Conflict is often a blend of light and dark moments. Humor is a valuable tool we use to cope. Finding the comedy in a sad or tragic event helps you gain perspective., and dispels emotional intensity. It can be what makes these memories bearable. Have you noticed the laughter at a funeral reception?

Many of the best-selling memoirs–*Angela's Ashes* by Frank McCourt or *Running with Scissors* by Augusten Burroughs–tell about heartbreaking events with wry humor.

We aren't saying that the event was in any way humorous. There is nothing funny about death or abuse or poverty. And yet, poking fun at what happened is a way to diminish the power of tragic events. Humor can reassert a sense of control over an uncontrollable situation. If you record a difficult time, it will prove more readable if sprinkled with some levity.

Whether conflict is big or small, public or private, our struggles make us real. Writing helps us make sense of them. This holds true, even if you are the only person who reads your work. Readers relate to real stories, to issues in which they can find meaning.

Take a deep breath. Have courage. And write.

THE BOY IN THE MIRROR
by Steve Cobb

Wood chips litter the shop floor.

The table saw whines down. "Looks clean," I say as I rub my hand across the edge of the 2 x 4 piece of wood. It's a Thursday morning, and I'm wasting time in shop class. I don't actually need to be here. But, I have two electives to complete if I'm going to graduate. I wisely chose food service as my second choice. The food is free.

As I prepare to run sandpaper across the edge of my freshly cut board, I turn, just in time to see him watching me, again. He's a junior. His name is John. He's also a loner–easy to pick on. I've said "hi" a couple times, nothing more. Seniors aren't supposed to interact with lower classmen, unless they have to. It's one of those unspoken rules. Personally, I don't give a shit.

"How's it going?" he says to me. I don't answer at first. Bill and Ted, two seniors, are standing nearby. Guilt tugs at my gut the longer I wait to say anything. "Good," I say, with a smile and a nod. He smiles back. At 5'9", athletic and husky, with a blond crop of hair trimmed neatly around his ears, he looks All-American. I wonder why he keeps trying with me.

When the bell rings I grab my books and head for the door.

"See ya later," he says as I walk by.

"Yeah, catch you later." I make eye contact, and for a split second, I see a reflection of myself.

At home that night I sit on my bed behind a locked door and ponder my future. I'm going to graduate in six months and it hits me that I have no future. My dad and I have waged war forever. Years of being told I couldn't do anything have taken their toll. I get up, go to the dresser, open the third drawer and pull out a tin box. Hidden under some playing cards is my only source of relief from the pain of loneliness that has gripped me since my sophomore year–my pipe and the small bag of weed, which is getting too low again. I stuff the goods in my coat pocket, run a comb through my curly brown hair, and head for the door. I've promised my friend Fred (who'd first introduced me to pot) I'd come over tonight.

The next day at school I spy John standing in the hallway. A couple of assholes walk by and knock the books out of his hands. He reaches down and picks them up. Ginger, our mutual petite blonde friend, runs up and grabs him by the arm. "You promised to go to the movies, remember?" John looks away.

Later in shop class I notice he's just standing around, watching the two guys that knocked his books to the floor.

I look over and try to make eye contact. He shoots me a look of rage that says, "Stay away. Don't come near." Later, I see him standing alone next to his locker. Just standing.

That night I toss and turn with his image in my mind.

The next day at school, Ginger is standing next to her locker, crying, while her friends try to console her.

I gently approach. "What's wrong?"

Ginger looks away. Her best friend Tina turns to me. "John killed himself last night. He used his dad's shotgun."

I feel like someone slugged me in the gut. The last image of John in shop class, standing alone with that angry expression on his face, haunts me for the rest of the day.

When I drive the noon food service run with Elsie, our blabbermouth cook who has to accompany us on the trips, our route takes us past John's house. Elsie cranes her neck as we drive by, "I heard they had to use a mop to clean up all the blood," she says.

When I get home that night, I go straight to my bedroom and look in the mirror.

The End

TEN

CREATING HERITAGE

> *Loss of continuity in the generations of our families is a tragic flaw in our society. Must each generation be rootless, denied knowledge of heritage?*
> LOIS DANIEL

Natalie is a widow in her eighties. She lives alone in an apartment, often watching game shows on television. Her children and grandchildren visit now and then. Would it surprise you to learn that she has a fascinating history?

Natalie was an attractive teen who lived in Poland during World War II. She was a Jew in a time when this was a dangerous thing. To survive, she escaped Poland and did the unthinkable: She pretended to be a Gentile, working in a German munitions factory under an assumed name. She could tell no one her real identity. Her few friendships with other factory girls were built on lies. For three and a half years, she lived in constant fear of being found out.

This story, while intriguing, has not yet been documented. Natalie comes from a generation that was not inclined to talk about the past. How many of us have relatives whose stories have never been recorded? As a result, our heritage is being lost.

But we can save it. We have the opportunity to document private history. Recording the life stories of another person can be challenging, but it is always worthwhile.

How do you tell someone else's story? Many people, especially seniors, are reluctant to write their stories but are often willing to answer questions. So ask questions. It could be an informal visit with a family member or a more formal interview. It's a good idea to jot down a few questions beforehand to direct the conversation. The following may launch the discussion:

1. Who was the first person who captured your heart?
2. What was the most difficult thing you've ever had to do?
3. How did you decide upon your career?
4. What accomplishment makes you most proud? When were you most disappointed?
5. How would you like to be remembered?
6. Describe your childhood home.
7. When were you the happiest? What made you the most sad?

Creating Heritage

8. Is there something about yourself that you think no one knows?

This list is not comprehensive. Use your imagination. What would you like to know about this person?

Although we call it an interview, it is just a conversation with an interesting person. Tape-record it, if possible. Inexpensive mini-recorders are available at most office supply stores. They have built-in microphones and are small enough to be unobtrusive. Place the microphone close to the subject and away from other noises.

During the interview, jot a few notes, if necessary, and ask for clarification if you are confused. Switch to a new question if the conversation stalls. But primarily, just let the person talk. Focus on listening. You will notice that, given time and encouragement, most people are natural storytellers. They will astound you with rich, poignant tales.

Barbara once interviewed her grandmother, Helen Farris, for more than eight hours over several sessions. As she transcribed the tapes, she was shocked by how often she had interrupted and redirected Helen in the midst of a story. Barbara wished she had just kept her mouth closed and her ears open. Nevertheless, she was able to uncover personal history about life during the Great Depression in the mining towns of Colorado. Prior to the interview, Helen had never before told many of these stories.

Once you have recorded the interview you have

several options. You can simply transcribe the tapes and have a written account of your interview. Or, to make the personal history more readable and interesting, you can transform the information into stories. Either way, that personal history is now preserved.

Digging for Details--Again We Nag

All good stories share one characteristic that makes them entertaining. Details. A reader might be able to imagine coming out of the cold into a comfortable kitchen, but it is infinitely easier if the writer tells you that bacon and fried onions sizzled in a skillet, and a wet, woolen scarf hung from a wooden peg on the wall. Vivid details help the reader picture what is taking place.

You have decided to write a story about your grandmother. You want to describe the way she lived and her personality.

Pointed questions about her should elicit specific information. For example,

- What color was Gran's house?
- Did she grow roses or daffodils?
- What did she eat for breakfast?
- What did her kitchen smell like? Fried chicken or chocolate cake?
- Describe several pieces of her furniture.
- Did she hang her laundry on the line?
- What was her favorite color?

- What perfume did she use?
- Did she have animals?
- What did she look like? Hair? Eye color? Stout? Thin?
- Did she use any expressions or nicknames?
- Name some activities that the two of you shared.
- Did she work or volunteer?
- What were her hobbies? (Knitting, bowling, cards?)

With this information, you can describe her with a few simple strokes. Consider:

"You pop out to the veranda, Skooks," Gran said, as she clumped across the kitchen floor in her black brogue pumps. "I've just squeezed some orange juice and I'll bring it out with your favorite tea biscuits."

In two sentences, you see how Gran moved and spoke, and you get a feeling for her relationship with her granddaughter.

The story is in the details. Paint a picture, rich to the senses.

Delving for the Dramatic

Another trait of good story telling is showing people interacting in a specific place, recording their dialogue. Which is more interesting:

Example A:
Johnny and Olivia had a huge fight in the middle of the ice cream parlor after he showed up late.

Example B:
Johnny sauntered into Drake's Ice Cream Parlor. He slid into the red leather-like bench next to Olivia and draped his arm around her shoulders.
Olivia pulled away. "You're late."
"Oh, babe, don't be mad." He leaned in for a kiss.
"Jerk!" Olivia dumped her ice cream on his head.

These techniques–detail, dialogue and dramatization --make any story stronger.

Inventing the Truth

In writing someone else's story, you are employing details and dialogue that belong to someone else. It's difficult to describe a scene when you weren't present. How do you record a conversation you never heard? How are you supposed to write a compelling story when you don't know what's "true?"

Keep in mind that anyone's recollection is already a "re-vision." People remember the gist of an event, the few details that stood out for them. It's the same with words. No one can recall the exact words used in conversation. The fact that your version of the "truth" is a revision of the original is an inescapable fact of recording an event secondhand.

As Barbara Kingsolver says, *"Memory is a complicated thing, a relative to truth, but not its twin."* When telling someone else's story, your responsibility is to convey the core truth of what happened. If possible, you ask questions of your subject to get accurate information. Sometimes you research a time period, including customs and fashions of the day. You find out how people spoke; the slang and idioms. You look at photographs to get a feel for an event. Having done your best to collect authentic information, you are still left with blank spaces that need to be filled in order to create a story. To fill these spaces, you may need to *invent the truth*.

Read "The Phone Call," a memoir by Phyllis Green printed at the end of this chapter. It is a family story and includes some of Phyllis's recollections of her grandmother. It also recreates events that happened before Phyllis was born. She has had to invent some details to bridge the gaps in the story handed down to her, but the core truth remains unchanged.

Taking the time to record the essence of someone else's story honors that person. It says that you believe a life is important and worth remembering as accurately as possible. As Bernard Selling wrote,

> *Ultimately, this is the great lure of life story writing: to be able to affect the future of the families into which we are born; to give direction, amusement and perspective to our children's children and their children; to write so*

well that a hundred years from now those who follow can clearly see the footprints we made and begin to guage their own paths by our direction."

Creating Heritage

THE PHONE CALL
by Phyllis Green

It is 1934. Sade Magill, once a redhead, but now with hair as pale as the November cornstalks, walks back to the house after feeding the pigs. She wipes her large hands on her flowered apron.
She hears the phone ring when she enters.
"Yes?"
"It's Alma."
"Who?"
"Alma."
"Well?"
"I just thought you ought to know. He's dead."

The Nursing Home
It is 1972. I am 40 years old. My father and I are visiting his mother (my grandmother, Grace) at a nursing home. When we arrive some helpers are giving my grandmother and her three roommates new hairdos. They have put a thin red ribbon in my grandmother's gray hair.

She knows my father but doesn't know me. We walk to a lounge with turquoise vinyl sofas where we can sit and chat.

Her short-term memory is gone but she tells many tales of when she was a girl on the farm. She talks about her mother a lot. She talks about her brothers and sisters. I recall she has always been a talker. At church she would be the last one to go home.

We spend an hour with her, then we kiss her goodbye. I will not see her for months because I live far away, but my father will spend every Sunday with her.

On the drive home, I say to my father, "Grandma speaks a lot about her mother but she never mentions her father."

I am shocked when he tells me her father left her mother and ten children to live with another woman twenty miles away.

The Meeting

It is 1934. I am two years old. There are a lot of people in the car. My father gets out several times to crank it. I sit on my mother's lap. I have on my navy wool coat and leggings, my white fur muff and white angora bonnet. A huge white bow in my brown hair sticks out of the bonnet.

When we get to the farm, I see a long brown box sitting in a surrey in the yard. Someone is at the outdoor pump getting water in a gray bucket. We enter a kitchen. There is a black stove. I can see flames inside. There is a tall woman in the kitchen. Her hair is pulled back in a bun just like my grandmother's.

This woman does not smile. She does not speak. Nor do I. I am pushed toward her.

"Your great-grandmother!" someone calls out.

We look at each other. It is the only time I have seen my great-grandmother, Sade Magill.

It is the day she brought him home to be buried on the farm.

The Promise

It is 1891. The time is 5 a.m. He crawls on top of her. Sade wakes with a little laugh. "Oh Johnny," she murmurs. Then alarmed she says, "Wait! Wait! You promised. The doctor stood right there," she says, pointing to a space beside the white chamber pot. "He said I'd bleed to death if I had another child. And you promised me, Johnny."

He does not go near her for three weeks. Then one day she finds him throwing clothes into an old feedbag.

"What are you doing?" she asks.

"I'm taking Thunder," he says gruffly. "I'll get him back to you in time for spring plantin'."

Creating Heritage

"How will I do plantin'? Maud and Grace are boy crazy. Little Sade and Mim are total crazy. Roger's but nine. The babies can't help."

She grabs the feedbag and throws out his underwear and shirts. They swirl about the room. She looks at her hands. They aren't as large as they will become.

John refills the feedbag with his stuff.

"Who is it?' she asks. "Who is she?"

"It's nothing like that," he replies. "It's a holiday. I'm taking a holiday." He puts on his black floppy hat.

She follows him outside.

He gets on the black horse, kicking its flank a bit so it trots out the gate. She runs after.

"Come back, you bastard!" she calls out.

He hears "BASTARD" as he rides past the Shrunk's white farmhouse and "BASTARD" again as he crosses over Emerson Creek.

The End

HALF PAST PERFECT

We are a species that needs and wants to understand who we are. Sheep lice do not seem to share this longing, which is one reason they write so little.
ANNE LAMOTT

Eleven

Now What?

> *[T]he unrecorded past is none other than our old friend, the tree in the primeval forest which fell where there was no one to hear the sound of the crash.*
> BARBARA TUCHMAN

Maybe by now, with introspection, perseverance and guts, you've written a story. You've printed it out, and it's lying on your desk. What are you supposed to do with it?

The next step is to decide if and how you want to share it. Some writers work with a plan for publication in mind from the first time they put pen to paper. Others know that a safe drawer is their goal; they write for themselves. Then there are all the other writers in between who want to share their stories but are looking for the right avenue.

The very act of sharing your work has value. After all, as Stephen King wrote, "[y]our stuff starts out being just for you ... but then it goes out. Once you know what the story is and get it right–as right as you can, anyway–it belongs to anyone who wants to read it."

Whether you think your stories will enlighten or entertain others, here are some options for sharing your work:

1. You decide to print one copy and you're done. That's okay. You may let others read it (we hope) but you have no interest in spreading your work to the far-flung corners of the Earth. This is a personal decision that appeals to many people as memoirs can be full of previously undisclosed facts that are difficult to make public. You might wish to place a clear plastic cover over each page to protect your work.

2. You might collect your stories in an album, similar to a photo album. You may even wish to include photos. This works well for those who wish to keep their stories for the eyes of family and friends, perhaps displaying your work on a coffee table or loaning it to those you trust. An album works well, too, if you only wish to make a few copies. The presentation can be handsome, inexpensive, and appropriate for gift-giving. Remember, *every* story is a gift.

3. How about a heritage newsletter? Unlike the popular holiday newsletters, which you may or may not appreciate,

Now What?

a heritage newsletter is more than a recitation of activities. Instead, it is a forum to share your family history. You could solicit contributions from parents or other relatives as well as your own tales. Whether you send it out quarterly or yearly, whether you use email or the postal service, this is one way to document and share your family history.

4. Instead of that tie or another pair of slippers, give someone the gift of a one-page story. Print it out in an interesting font on good paper and sign it. Your signature is a precious addition. Then frame it. This gift will outlast a box of chocolates and have more meaning.

5. Start a family web page as a central repository for posting and exchanging stories. Several Internet service providers (ISP's) host free web sites that can be used for this purpose. Your teenager could use it as a blogging site. Great Aunt Mary may not be on the Net, but her story can be. This is also a place to post pictures.

6. Start a family story night. Designate one evening a month to gather for the purpose of sharing tales. Each family member could bring a short story to read aloud. Your teenage daughter may roll her eyes and tell you she'd rather wash her hair. Your ten-year-old may be distracted by a video game. You might have to resort to bribery. Here's a tip: Start with your own stories about your childhood. Write about a time when you felt awkward or foolish. Kids love to hear about their parents' mistakes. At the end of the evening, place the stories in a binder. Imagine the marvelous collection of written family history that would

accumulate over the years.

7. Form a life story club. There are book clubs, gourmet clubs, ya-ya gatherings–all based on passions that bring people together for fun and enriching experiences. Finding ways to share the stories of your life is a compelling reason to get together with others. Friends gather, perhaps in your living room. Each guest brings a short story to share with the group. You might have a theme for these evenings: births, deaths, a favorite childhood toy. Serve a lovely beverage and yummy finger food. People love to talk about themselves, love to have others listen. You are creating a community through story. You might want to gather the tales in a binder.

8. Your stories can be published for the general public. One avenue is e-publishing. It is a less expensive option than traditional book publishing. You can search the Internet for an e-publisher and get your stories on-line. This is a new industry and not well-regulated. Some companies produce your work as a CD. Some create a down-loadable file. Some will digitally print your work as a book. Always read the fine print of any company with whom you decide to do business. Some e-publishers are royalty-paying, honest companies. Some are not. Be careful.

9. You might want to present your work to a traditional book or magazine publisher. This is a long journey that begins with submitting a polished manuscript to a publisher (as all the memoir writers you have read obviously did with success). To send a manuscript to a

Now What?

traditional publisher, go to the library or a bookstore and consult a writer's market guide to see which firms are currently accepting manuscripts in this genre. Obtain the submission guidelines. We suggest you research royalty and book rights information for each publisher you contact. There are many good resources available to teach you how to navigate this process. Who knows, you could be the next Maya Angelou or Frank McCourt.

10. One publishing option particularly attractive to memoir writers is self–publishing, which is spending your own money to produce your work in book form. Self-publishing is not the same as "vanity" publishing, which is paying an inflated price to produce and promote your book, sharing royalties with the publisher.

Instead, there are companies that will produce and print your work while you retain total control. Many well-known books–including Mark Twain's *The Adventures of Huckleberry Finn*, Richard Bolles' *What Color is Your Parachute*, *The Elements of Style* by Strunk & White, and *A Time to Kill* by John Grisham–were self-published. Because of recent advancements in computer and printing technology, this option is becoming more feasible and cost-effective. Not only is your work bound and presented in the most professional manner, but you will be proud to give your book to family and friends or sell to bookstores. Doing your research and price shopping are critical in wading through the choices. For information, check our web page at www.pastperfectstories.com.

Weigh your presentation options carefully. Base your decision on your goals. It is most important that you enjoy your stories.

Barbara's story "Moonshine," printed at the end of this chapter, was one of several stories she wrote about her grandmother's experiences living in the mining towns. As a Christmas present for her grandmother, Barbara collected the stories along with historic photos and published several hardbound copies.

Her grandmother enjoyed the book and placed it on the coffee table of her living room. This was Barbara's purpose in writing. But then, something else happened. Now that the stories were printed, other family members read them. Many had never heard about the events the book recounted.

However you decide to present your work, we encourage you to share it. You may never know how many people will be affected by your work.

Happy Printing!

Now What?

MOONSHINE
by Barbara Allen Burke

On October 28, 1919, Congress passed the National Prohibition Act.

Four-year-old Helen didn't know about Prohibition and didn't care. Other matters loomed large. Her mother, Mabel, a stout, ruddy-faced woman, sat Helen down at the kitchen table one morning, stirred precious sugar into her coffee, and explained that Uncle Frank had died. Helen didn't know what that meant except that Aunt Jessie, Frank's widow, and their daughters, Edna and Maxine, were coming to live with them.

After Jessie and the girls moved in, Helen noticed that strange people came often to their house, handing Jessie fistfuls of cash for a liquid poured into dark glass bottles and old canning jars. When she asked her aunt about the bottles, she was told it was secret.

"What's in Jessie's bottles, Mama?" Helen asked Mabel.

Mabel lifted a loaf of bread out of the oven. "It ain't nothing you need to fuss over," she said. "Just hand me that towel before I burn myself."

One clear spring afternoon, Mabel shooed the girls out the door. "You're under foot," she said. "Play outside."

Helen, Edna and Maxine spilled out of the house into the flat dirt yard. They played Ring 'Round the Rosy, tripping over their long skirts and petticoats, falling in the dirt until all three were smudged and smiling.

Aunt Jessie came running up the street, lifting her skirts high enough to show her booted feet. She ran past the girls and burst into the house.

"Mabel, you got to help me hide the bootleg," she yelled. "The

Agents are coming!"

The girls scrambled to their feet and followed Jessie inside, watching the women scurry about the kitchen, squirreling bottles and jars into cardboard boxes.

"I'll never be able to hide all of this," Jessie seethed.

Edna called from the doorway. "What's the matter, Mama?"

Jessie stopped, a dark green bottle in each hand, and stared at the girls as if she'd only just noticed them. And then she smiled.

"The girls!" she cried. "That's it!"

Mabel kept packing boxes. "What fool thing are you talking about now?"

Jessie ignored her. "Girls, follow me."

She grabbed a box clinking with bottles and carried it to the yard. She set it on the ground and settled Edna on top, carefully arranging the girl's skirts and petticoats.

By the time the agents marched up the street, Edna, Helen and Maxine sat in a small circle in the front yard, perched like hens atop hidden boxes of bootleg whiskey. They played a clapping game, careful not to disturb their overburdened skirts.

Pease porridge hot. Pease porridge cold.

Pease porridge in the pot, nine days old.

The agents, five dour men with dark hats, tramped past the girls, up the porch steps, and pounded on the front door. They carried axes. One carried a gun. "It's a raid!" they yelled, and pushed through the door. The girls kept clapping.

Some like it hot. Some like it cold.

Some like it in the pot, nine days old.

The men searched the house, overturning mattresses, emptying cupboards, spilling a bag of flour on the floor. They upended a wooden chest and dumped a laundry basket. Still the girls clapped.

Pease porridge hot. Pease porridge cold.

Pease porridge in the pot, nine days old.

Finally, the agents left, glaring at Jessie as they stomped away. One man looked back. "I know you're up to something, missy." He

Now What?

almost ran into the circle of girls. He sidestepped to avoid them, and followed the other men down the street.

For years, even after Jessie got a job as a waitress in Denver and she and the girls moved away, Helen couldn't hear that clapping rhyme without thinking of dark green bottles of bootleg.

The End

*Writing became such a process
of discovery that I couldn't wait
to get to work in the morning.
I wanted to know what I was
going to say.*
SHARON O'BRIEN

Twelve

The Last Word

> *Write your story as it needs to be written. Write it honestly, and tell it as best you can. I'm not sure that there are any other rules. Not ones that matter.*
> NEIL GAIMAN

In this book, we've presented a simple way to retrieve your memories and pin them to paper in the form of small stories. The "little bits of wisdom" we introduced at the beginning of this book have now come full circle. Remember . . .

Your Stories are Unique and Worth Telling.

Your stories preserve a piece of history that will otherwise be lost. These stories also explore what you've done, where you've been and what you've learned along the way. No one else can record your life as honestly as you can.

Everyone Can Write.
Using Lifelines, you'll be surprised how many stories crowd to the front of your mind, begging to be written. With Lifelines, Story Starters, and Play-Write techniques, everyone can write an entertaining tale. As Robert Cormier said, "[t]he beautiful part of writing is that you don't have to get it right the first time, unlike, say, a brain surgeon." Writing is not brain surgery. Have fun with it.

Writing Clarifies What You Find Meaningful.
Your recognition and understanding of meaningful moments in your life become more apparerent when you see your stories on paper. In writing, you realize the power you have to control how your life is presented to others.

Life Writing Restores Your Past.
Re-storying your past brings you face to face with attitude and choice because you get to tell your story your way. With every stroke of the pen, you have the opportunity to change past attitudes and choices in order to see your life in a more positive light.

Small Stories Are Powerful.
You live your life in single moments, any of which can hold great meaning. A significant event can be forever captured in a several paragraphs or pages. Never underestimate the impact of a few words on paper.

The Last Word

Anyone Can Publish.
Publishing is not just for famous people. Consider it a viable option through which to communicate your stories. It doesn't matter how you share your work. It's just important that you do.

In your writing journey, you will make another delightful discovery: Gratitude is born in the mining of memories and the writing of stories. Spending time with the people of your past, remembering the experiences you've treasured, reminds you of the countless moments you've already lived. Life story writing allows you to revisit those amazing times and to appreciate them. A new respect for your past may invite gratitude to enter your stories. As Melody Beattie wrote,

> *Gratitude makes sense of our past, brings peace for today, and creates a vision for tomorrow.*

"A Daughter Walking Away," the final story at the end of this chapter, is a mother's reflection on her relationship with her daughter. Although the letter's purpose is to share whatever wisdom she might have gathered over the years, the underlying voice of the story is one of immense gratitude for the relationship.

You have the tools you need to put stories on paper. What do you have to say? As the writer of your life, you have the last word.

The End

The Last Word

A DAUGHTER WALKING AWAY
by Barbara Allen Burke

Dear Katherine–

How could I not know, when I first held you in my arms almost eighteen years ago, that this day would come. I wasn't looking forward enough. And yet tomorrow we drive into Boston and help you move into the first place where you will live without me. We'll set up your pink mixer in your kitchen, hang the shower curtain in your bathroom, and set up your desk. We'll buy groceries and hang pictures on the wall. Eventually, after a bit of sightseeing and a few meals, I'll leave and go back home. And you will stay in Boston, such a long, long way from where I live and work and sleep. I'll have to get used to a life I haven't known since before you were born. I wasn't really prepared. But I don't know how you prepare yourself for this. Maybe you can't.

You have always had a way of pushing me faster than I felt I was ready to go. And yet, I have to say, it was thrilling, in the way that a roller coaster leaves you breathless but exhilarated; the terrifying turns, staggering drops, and dizzying views from the top. I realize now that so much of my life turned around riding that roller coaster with you. You were such a joy! You were always by my side, looking at me with those steady, hazel eyes, expecting good things, helping me believe that it would all, in the end, be all right. And now, the roller coaster has rolled into the station and I am stepping out of the car to watch your ride from the ground, and to participate from a distance. A great distance.

I guess I am both thankful and sad. I don't really have any regrets (well, not too many at least). I've made mistakes that I hope you will forgive. Like not letting you read Nancy Drew books when you were eight. You are a great daughter, and more importantly, a solid, caring person. You have strong values, a big heart, and a good *mind. You are beautiful and charming and fun. You seem to have a passion for your life, which is more than any mother can hope for. You will be fine, I know. More than fine. You have a great life in front of you and I am so excited to watch it unfold and know that I get to take part.*

Now, just so you don't forget:

- *You are in charge of what you say, what you think, and what you do.*
- *You are only in charge of what you say, what you think, and what you do.*
- *Floss, even though you don't want to. Someday you will be glad you took care of your teeth.*
- *In dealing with other people, be respectful and honest.*
- *Drink lots of milk.*
- *You are being led toward your best life, even though the path is not always obvious.*
- *You become what you believe. What you focus on expands. So focus on the positive aspects of your life, and find good things to believe in.*
- *Drive safely.*
- *Find joy in little things—flowers in a vase, a nice candle, the smell of rain, snow.*
- *And, to quote a movie line, "Make good choices."*

I love you always,
Mom

The End

BIBLIOGRAPHY

Acton, Lord John. "Inaugural Lecture," quoted in Wallace, Tricia, "Lord Acton: The History of Liberty." Loyola University History Department web page: www.loyno.edu.history/journal/1991-92/wallace.htm#23.

Barrington, Judith. 2002. *Writing the Memoir: From Truth to Art.* Portland: The Eighth Mountain Press.

Barrington, Judith. "Surrounded By Lies." *The Oregonian,* January 29, 2006.

Beattie, Melody. [1987] 1992. *Codependent No More.* Center City, MN: Hazelden.

Berry, Wendell. [1983] 2005. *Standing by Words: Essays.* Emeryville, CA: Shoemaker & Hoard.

Conway, Jill Ker. "Points of Departure," in Zinsser, william (Ed.). 1998. *Inventing the Truth: The Art and Craft of Memoir.* New York: Houghton Mifflin Company.

Cormier, Robert. Quoted on Brainy Quotes webpage: www.brainyquotes.com/authors/r/robert_cormier.html.

Daniel, Lois. 1985. *How to Write Your Own Life Story : A Step by Step Guide for the Non-Professional Writer.* Chicago: Chicago Review Press.

Davis, Donald, as quoted in Maguire, Jack, 1998. *The Power of Personal Storytelling.* New York: Tarcher/Putnam.

Dinesen, Isak. [1979] 1984. *Daguerrotypes and Other Essays.* Chicago: University of Chicago Press.

Doig, Ivan, [1978] 1992. *This House of Sky.* Orlando: Harcourt Brace & Co.

Forster, E. M. 1956. *Aspects of a Novel*. New York: Harcourt Brace Jovanich.

Frankl, Victor E. [1959, 1962] 1984. *Man's Search for Meaning*. New York: Washington Square Press.

Fulgham, Robert. [1986] 1988. *All I Really Need to Know I Learned in Kindergarten*. New York: Villard Books.

Gaiman, Neil. "The Day I Was Interviewed by Maddy." *Neil Gaiman Online Journal*, June 15, 2004. At www.neilgaiman.com/journal/2004/06/day-i-was-interviewed-by-maddy.asp.

Ghandi, Mohandas. *The Ghandi Foundation of USA Web Page* at www.gandhifoundationusa.com/quotes.htm.

Graham, Martha, quoted in De Mille, Agnes. [1952] 1980. *Dance to the Piper*. New York: Da Capo Press.

Ionesco, Eugene. 1964. *Notes and Counter Notes*. New York: Grove Press.

Keleman, Stanley. Quoted in the Quote Garden web page at www.quotegarden.com/history.html.

Kingsolver, Barbara, as quoted in Maguire, Jack. 1998. *The Power of Personal Storytelling*. New York: Tarcher/Putnam.

Lamott, Anne. 1994. *Bird by Bird: Some Instructions on Writing and Life*. New York: Anchor Books.

Lawrence, D. H., as quoted on web page for University of North Caroline Writing Center: www.unco.edu/english/wcenter/quotes.htm.

Lejeune, Philippe. "The Autobiographical Pact." In P. J. Eakin (Ed.). [1985] 1989. *On Autobiography* (K. Leary, Trans.). Minneapolis: University of Minnesota Press, 1989. In Daniel Schacter and Elaine Scarry (Eds.). 2001. *Memory, Brain and Belief*. Cambridge, Mass.: Harvard University Press.

Maguire, Jack. 1998. *The Power of Personal Storytelling*. New York: Tarcher/Putnam.

Mairs, Nancy. 1995. *Remembering the Bone House: An Erotics of Place and Space*. Boston: Beacon Press.

McClelland, James. "Constructive Memory and Memory Distortions: A Parallel-Distributed Processing Approach.

In D. L. Schacter (ed.), 1995. *Memory Distortion: How Minds, Brains, and Societies Reconstruct the Past.* Cambridge, Mass: Harvard University Press.

Metzger, Deena. 1992. *Writing for Your Life.* San Francisco: HarperSanFrancisco.

Moore, Robin. 1991. *Awakening the Hidden Storyteller.* Boston: Sambhala, as quoted in Maguire, Jack, 1998. *The Power of Personal Storytelling.* New York: Jeremy P. Tarcher/Putnam.

O'Brien, Sharon. Quoted on About.com web page: quotations. about.com/cs/inspirationquotes/a/writing1.htm.

Paglia, Camille. Quoted on QuotationsBook.com webpage: www.quotationsbook.com/authors/5522/camille_paglia.

Parry, Alan and Doan, Robert E. 1994. *Story Revisions: Narrative Therapy in the Postmodern World.* New York: The Guilford Press.

Ranpura, Ashish. "How We Remember, and Why We Forget," www.brainconnection.com/topics/?main=fa/memory-formation, June 2000.

Sacks, Oliver. 1987. *The Man Who Mistook His Wife for a Hat, and Other Clinical Tales.* New York: Harper.

Schacter., D. L. 2001. *The Seven Sins of Memory: How the Mind Forgets and Remembers.* Cambridge, Mass: Harvard University Press.

Selling, Bernard. 1988. *Writing from Within: A Guide to Creativity and Life Story Writing.* Alameda, CA: Hunter House, Inc.

Shakespeare, William. From *The Tempest.* 1974. *The Riverside Shakespeare.* Boston: Houghton Mifflin Company.

Slater, Lauren. 1996. *Welcome to My Country: A Therapist's Memoir of Madness.* New York: Random House.

Smith, Jimmy Neil (Ed.). 1988. *Homespun,* as quoted in Maguire, Jack. 1998. *The Power of Personal Storytelling.* New York: Tarcher/Putnam.

Stotter, Ruth., (Ed.). 1995. *One Hundred Memorable Quotes About Stories and Storytelling.* Stinson Beach, CA: Stotter Press, as quoted in Maguire, Jack. 1998. *The Power of Personal Storytelling.* New York: Tarcher/Putnam.

Sylvester, Robert, as quoted by Covino, Jennifer in "What brain-based research means for educators and for the future of math, language arts, foreign language, the arts and special education," www.districtadministration.com/page.cfm?id=235.

Taylor, Daniel. 1996. *The Healing Power of Stories.* New York: Doubleday, as quoted in Maguire, Jack. 1998. *The Power of Personal Storytelling.* New York: Tarcher/Putnam.

Tuchman, Barbara. 1982. *Practicing History: Selected Essays.* New York: Ballantine Books.

Webster's II New Riverside Dictionary, Revised Edition. 1996. New York: Houghton Mifflin Company.

Weil, Simone. [1952] 2002. *The Need for Roots: Prelude to a Declaration of Duties Toward Mankind, Second Edition.* New York: Routledge.

Westbury, Chris & Dennett, Daniel, "Mining the Past to Construct the Future: Memory and Belief as Forms of Knoweldge," as quoted in Schacter, D. and Scarry, Elaine (Eds). 2001. *Memory, Brain and Belief.* Cambridge, Mass.: Harvard University Press.

Wolff, Tobias, quoted in Sittenfeld, Curtis. "The Writing Obsession," *The Atlantic Online,* November 12, 2003.

Zinsser, William, Ed., 1987. *Inventing the Truth: The Art and Craft of Memoir.* Boston: Houghton Mifflin.

RECOMMENDED READING LIST

Memoirs and Biographies:

Adams, Henry. [1918] 1931. *The Education of Henry Adams.* New York: Modern Library.

Angelou, Maya. [1970] 1997. *I Know Why the Caged Bird Sings.* New York: Bantam.

Baker, Russell. 1982. *Growing Up.* New York: Signet.

Barrington, Judith. 2000. *Lifesaving: A Memoir.* Portland, OR: Eighth Mountain Press.

Beck, Martha. 1999. *Expecting Adam.* New York: Times Books.

Bragg, Rich. 1998. *All Over But the Shoutin'.* New York: Vintage.

Jill Ker Conway. 1990. *The Road from Coorain.* New York: Vintage.

Dillard, Annie. 1982. *Teaching a Stone to Talk:* New York: Harper Perennial.

----------. 1987. *An American Childhood.* New York: Harper & Row.

Doig, Ivan. 1978. *This House of Sky: Landscapes of a Western Mind.* New York: Harcourt Brace & Company.

Duncan, David James. 1995. *River Teeth: Stories and Writings.* New York: Bantam Books.

Eggers, David. 2000. *A Heartbreaking Work of Staggering Genius: Based on a True Story.* New York: Simon & Schuster.

Frankl, Victor E. [1959] 1984. *Man's Search for Meaning.* New York: Washington Square Press.

Fisher, M. F. K. [1937] 2004. *The Art of Eating.* Hoboken, NJ: Wiley Publications.

Lamott, Anne. 2005. *Plan B: More Thoughts on Faith.* New York: Riverhead Books.

----------. 1999. *Traveling Mercies: Some Thoughts on Faith.* New York: Pantheon Books.

Karr, Mary. 1995. *The Liars' Club: A Memoir.* New York: Penguin.

Kazin, Alfred. [1946] 1969. *A Walker in the City.* Orlando, FL: Harcourt.

Kingston, Maxine Hong. 1977. *The Woman Warrior: Memoirs of a Girlhood Among Ghosts.* New York: Vintage.

Rosenthal, Amy Krauss. 2005. *Encyclopedia of an Ordinary Life.* New York: Three Rivers Press.

Lewis, C. S. 1955. *Surprised by Joy: The Shape of My Early Life.* New York: Harcourt, Brace & World.

McBride, James. 1996. *The Color of Water: A Black Man's Tribute to His White Mother.* New York: Riverhead Books.

Maclean, Norman. 1989. *A River Runs Through It.* Chicago: University of Chicago Press.

Mairs, Nancy. 1995. *Remembering the Bone House: An Erotics of Place and Space.* Boston: Beacon Press.

Mayes, Frances. 1996. *Under the Tuscan Sun: At Home in Italy.* New York: Broadway Books.

McCourt, Frank. 1996. *Angela's Ashes.* New York: Scribner.

----------. 1999. *'Tis: A Memoir.* New York: Touchstone.

Nabokov, Vladimir. [1947] 1967. *Speak, Memory.* New York: Vintage International.

Rawicz, Slavomir. [1956] 1997. *The Long Walk: The True Story of a Trek to Freedom.* Guildford, Conn.: The Lyons Press.

Saint-Exupéry, Antoine de. 1939. *Wind, Sand and Stars.* New York: Harcourt Brace & Company.

Stafford, Kim. 2002. *Early Mornings: Remembering my Father, William Stafford.* St. Paul, MN: Graywolf Press.

Stegner, Wallace. 1992. *Where the Bluebird Sings to the Lemonade Springs: Living and Writing in the West.* New York: Penguin Books.

Tan, Amy. 2003. *The Opposite of Fate: Memories of a Writing Life.* New York: Penguin Books.

Thoreau, Henry David. [1854] 1995. *Walden; or, Life in the Woods.* New York: Dover Publications.

Twain, Mark. [1883] 2001. *Life on the Mississippi*. New York: Signet.

Vidal, Gore. 1995. *Palimpsest: A Memoir.* New York: Random House.

Weisel, Elie. [1972] 2006. *Night. Translated by Marion Weisel. New York: Hill and Wang.*

Whitman, Walt. [1955] 1980. *Leaves of Grass. New York: The New American Library, Inc.*

Wolff, Tobias. 1989. *This Boy's Life.* New York: Harper & Row.

Books on Writing

Barrington, Judith. 2002. *Writing the Memoir: From Truth to Art.* Portland: The Eighth Mountain Press.

Bradbury, Ray. 1990. *Zen in the Art of Writing.* Santa Barbara, CA: Capra Press.

Cameron, Julia. [1992] 2002. *The Artist's Way: A Spiritual Path to Higher Creativity.* New York: Tarcher/Putnam.

----------. 1998. *The Right to Write.* New York: Tarcher/Putnam.

Daniel, Lois. *How to Write Your Own Life Story: A Step by Step Guide for the Non-Professional Writer*

Heilbrun, Carolyn G. 1988. *Writing a Woman's Life.* New York: Ballantine Books

King, Stephen. 2000, *On Writing: A Memoir of the Craft.* New York: Scribner.

Lamott, Anne. 1994. *Bird by Bird: Some Instructions on Writing and Life.* New York: Anchor Books.

Selling, Bernard. 1998. *Writing from Within: A Guide to Creativity and Life Story Writing.* Alameda, CA: Hunter House Publishers.

Spence, Linda. 1997. *Legacy: A Step-by-Step Guite to Writing Personal History.* Athens, Ohio: Swallow Press/Ohio University Press.

Strunk, Jr., William and White, E. B. 1979. *Elements of Style.* New

York: Macmillan Publishing Co., Inc.

Welty, Eudora. 1984. *One Writer's Beginnings.* Cambridge, MA: Harvard University Press.

Zinsser, William. 1987. *Inventing the Truth: The Art and Craft of Memoir.* Boston: Houghton Mifflin.

----------. [1976] 1998. *On Writing Well.* New York: HarperCollins.

----------. 2004. *Writing About Your Past: A Journey Into the Past.* New York: Marlowe & Company

About the Authors

Elizabeth Taylor has published three young adult/middle reader novels. She believes in kindness to people and animals, and the preservation of stories. Elizabeth writes, speaks and instructs classes in life writing. She lives in Lake Oswego, Oregon, with her husband, Michael, her two daughters, Tess and Annabelle, Miss Daisy the Golden Retriever, and Boo-Boo Kitty.

Barbara Allen Burke is a writer, teacher and counselor. In addition to writing fiction, she has worked with memoir writing for the past twelve years. She lives in Lake Oswego, Oregon, with her husband, Doug, and has four children: Katherine, Sam, Kate and Sarah. Some of her favorite memories involve long talks over coffee, traveling with her family, and connecting to people through story.

Order Form

Name

Address

City/State   Zip/Postal Code

Phone   Country (outside of U.S.)

Title	Qty.	Price	Total
Half Past Perfect		@ $14.95	
Half Past Perfect Story Starter		@ $ 9.95	
Combo-Pack: *Half Past Perfect* AND *Half Past Perfect Story Starter*		@ $23.75	
Shipping/Handling: First Book: $4.00 ($4.50 outside U.S.) Each additional book: $3.00 Combo-Pack: $5.75	Total Shipping & Handling Total Enclosed *Please pay in U.S. funds only.* *Make check payable to* *"Z-Story Press"*		

Complete and mail to:

Z-Story Press

P. O. Box 284, Lake Oswego, Oregon 97034

Phone: (503) 319-4047 or (503) 314-6848

Or order from our website at **www.z-storypress.com**

Prices subject to change without notice.